How to Study Psychology

Do you want to spend less time studying but end up with better grades, and a deeper understanding of the subject?

Studying psychology is a skill that can be learned. In this unique and practical 'how to' guide, Warren Davies offers some simple techniques that will enable students to keep information in, organise their workload, and be more productive. By applying some simple and easy-to-make changes to your study habits, you'll learn how to:

- get more work done in less time
- use memory techniques to help you breeze through exams
- beat procrastination
- develop a deep grasp of difficult topics
- write excellent essays (including how to avoid the seven most common essay errors)
- write a dissertation to publishable standard
- understand the 'results' section of research papers
- cut your study time in half.

This book is written specifically with psychology undergraduate students in mind, and as such will enhance your learning and improve your grades with techniques that actually work.

Warren Davies is a freelance writer with a background in psychology. He finished his Bachelor's degree in psychology in 2008 and a Masters in applied positive psychology in 2011. He is interested in the factors that affect human performance and well-being and is one of those weird people who actually enjoys statistics.

How to Study Psychology

Warren Davies

Ψ Psychology Press
Taylor & Francis Group

LONDON AND NEW YORK

Published 2013
by Psychology Press
27 Church Road, Hove, East Sussex BN3 2FA

Simultaneously published in the USA and Canada
by Psychology Press
711 Third Avenue, New York, NY 10017

*Psychology Press is an imprint of the Taylor & Francis Group, an informa
business*

British Library Cataloguing in Publication Data
A catalogue record for this book is available from the British Library

Library of Congress Cataloging-in-Publication Data
Davies, Warren.
  How to study psychology / Warren Davies.
    p. cm.
1. Psychology—Study and teaching.   I. Title.
BF77.D38 2012
150.71—dc23
                                    2012021443

ISBN: 978-1-84872-106-7 (pbk)
ISBN: 978-0-20307-937-9 (ebk)

Typeset in Times New Roman
by RefineCatch Limited, Bungay, Suffolk

MIX
Paper from
responsible sources
FSC   **FSC® C004839**
www.fsc.org

Printed and bound in Great Britain by
TJ International Ltd, Padstow, Cornwall

Thanks to

Vera Hegarty
UEL MAPPsters
Akem Singh
Mum
Lyndsey
Sue
Grandma

Contents

List of Figures

List of Tables

1 Introduction

Welcome to this study guide for psychology students. I think I know something about you. Since you have bought this book, I'm fairly safe in assuming you're a psychology student. If not, you're almost certainly studying a science of some sort and you perhaps feel a little tinge of anxiety about whether this book is applicable to your subject (don't worry – it is). As a student, money is a little tight for you and you're hoping this was a good investment (don't worry – it was).

What else do I know about you? I might deduce that you're one of the people who actually cares about their course and you want to get something out of it. You bought or otherwise obtained a study guide, after all. You want a good grade; you have a career goal in psychology or maybe you're just the type of person who likes to do a good job in everything they do. Maybe you're already doing fairly well on the course but you feel some motivation to do better. This is not the first study guide you've read, is it? It's OK, I'm not the jealous type; you can read around.

Or maybe I've mistaken you for someone else. You're on the eve of a deadline or your exams are looming. You bought this book to help you get through this ordeal alive! Left it all to the last minute again, didn't you? Don't worry; everyone does that. But, you've bought a study guide; that means you care. You have ambition in you. Admit it: you secretly believe you're capable of doing really well on this course. I bet sometimes, when you're on the train or the bus, you even allow yourself to daydream about getting top marks. It's OK, your secret is safe with me. By the way, de-clutter your desk – you'll feel better.

Whoever you are, you feel pressured sometimes. There's a lot to do on this course, isn't there? It feels like there's so much to remember, so much to do and so little time! Sometimes it's hard to find a balance between studying and having a social life. Sometimes you have to make a choice between the two. Social life usually wins but you wish you could have both. That's part of your motivation in buying this book – you want to do well academically without sacrificing your personal life – or vice-versa!

Have I described you? Maybe I haven't pinpointed you exactly but you recognize bits of yourself here and there. So as you sit there, hopefully having made the decision to put this book at the top of your 'to read' list (which is the right decision, incidentally), let me thank you for your purchase and express my hope that this book won't end up on your 'books to read later' list.

The philosophy behind this book

If you break a task down into its constituent parts, then figure out better, quicker or more efficient ways of doing those individual parts, you can improve your performance on the overall task. The organization of this book is based on my subjective breakdown of what is fundamentally involved in studying for a psychology degree and a collection of different ways you can improve within each of these areas.

But, we're all different. Not everything in these pages will appeal to you – or work for you – in your specific situation. If you're struggling with a particular class or aspect of studying in general, figure out where the problem lies, within the areas I'll describe, and try to fix it using some of the suggestions. Customize: try things out, notice the results and feel free to modify and adapt the ideas as you go. As Bruce Lee famously said: 'Absorb what is useful, reject what is useless, and add what is specifically your own.'

How the book is broken down

I have broken down the studying process in psychology into seven main sections. These are:

- Foundation knowledge:
  - ○ Research methods in psychology
  - ○ Statistics
- Study skills:
  - ○ Getting information in
  - ○ Keeping information in
  - ○ Understanding information
  - ○ Getting information out
  - ○ Organization and productivity.

Most of these are self-explanatory. After getting an understanding of the foundations of the field (trust me: they're not as scary as you might think), we move on to actual study skills; how to find, not forget, and understand the information you need for your course. Getting information out gives you strategies and tips for your written assignments and exams and the final section explains how you can make better use of your time.

How to use this book

If you want to read this book cover to cover, you certainly can. But it's not necessary to read it in that way. You are supposed to read it all but the order is up to you. It's a reference book, leave it on your desk, coffee table or even in your bathroom – I don't mind. Just refer to it regularly and try to read whole sections at a time.

To start with, I recommend that you skim through the book and the contents and identify the sections that you think are most pertinent to you. Then read those first. If you're doing research for an essay, go to page 51. If you're having trouble understanding something, go to page 73. And so on.

If you're reading this book linearly, we're going to start by looking at research methods and statistics. I know, I know, you probably hate them. But don't worry, we're not going into too much depth and there are no scary equations or anything like that. This stuff is the foundation of your subject and it will be a huge advantage for you to – at the very least – get a broad understanding of why all this stuff needs to be a part of the study of the mind and behaviour. But I hope to give you a bit more than that.

2   Research methods in psychology

Richard Feynman once said 'Social science is an example of a science that is not a science. They follow the forms; you gather data, you do so and so [to it] ... but they don't get any laws! They haven't got anywhere. Yet.' If I was there at the time Feynman said that, I might have debated the point with him. Since he was a Nobel prize-winning genius, I'd have lost, of course; but that's not the point. In my view, a field isn't classed as a science based on whether it has discovered any laws but, rather, on whether they 'follow the forms.' In other words, whether they use the scientific method to try to find out about the world.

Much to the dismay of many first-year psych students, fresh with enthusiasm from the latest episode of *Profiler* or *Lie to Me*, psychology does use the scientific method. So, if you want to understand the field or do well in your course, the first step is to build an understanding of what science is, what it is not, and why. This feels like the donkey work for most people and maybe you'd rather get stuck into theories of behaviour than the philosophy of science. However, the scientific method is the foundation on which all that other stuff is built. If you don't get a handle on this, you will:

- find every journal you read difficult to understand
- be liable to make mistakes in your work and have a weaker grasp of the subject
- get lower marks than your classmates who do understand it
- become more frustrated as time goes on.

But if you do get a grasp of this, you will:

- be able to understand journal papers more easily
- be able to criticize studies and theories more easily – which is essential if you want to get a good grade
- have a better grasp of the field as a whole
- have the edge over your peers, most of whom do not have this knowledge (you do know you are graded relative to your classmates, don't you?).

If you've seen *The Matrix*, you'll remember the scene where Neo finally saw the matrix for what it was; from that point on, everything changed for him. That's what you'll be like when you understand these foundations. Everything will just make sense. You're *The One!* And you don't need to be a Nobel prizewinner to get these benefits either. Just a basic grasp will be enough and these sections will give you that. I'm not going to tell you how to do all the calculations and analyses, only how to understand journal papers. So don't worry; the technical terms might seem complicated at first but you'll get used to them and there's no maths or calculation to do (I promise!).

The truth of the matter

All scientists, including psychologists, are seeking 'the truth'. Like most people, they believe that there is an objective world 'out there', in which we all live, and that having accurate information about this world is 'a good thing'. These are pretty much the only assumptions scientists make.

So what's the best way to find out about the world? Well, we could make some observations and jot them down. That could work. But what if you observe one thing and I observe something else? Or what if we observe the same thing but interpret it differently? We both have our own perceptions, biases and, perhaps, even reasons to lie. How would a third person determine, to the highest level of accuracy, which one of us was right?

What is science?

Science is simply a tool, a system that people use to get around problems like the one above. Every rule and procedure of the scientific method exists because it is the best way we currently know to get *objective* information about the world and to get around problems like our biases, propensity to lie and inaccurate perceptions. What scientists are looking for, specifically, are cause and effect relationships between different things (the technical term for 'thing' being variable).

But the scientific method is not always followed so precisely. Even with all the rules and procedures that have been devised, it is not a perfect system. That's why you need to know the rules so you can see when they've been broken. Scientists are human and this does happen, particularly, you might argue, in psychology. When these different rules are broken, it calls the results of a study ever-so-slightly into question. The bigger the rule that is broken, the more suspect are the results. You need to be able to recognize this.

You also need to know the rules so that you can weigh up the evidence of competing theories. Very often, there are two or more different theories claiming to explain the same thing. You might look at the research for these theories and think 'In these studies they did not select participants randomly; in this one they didn't use enough participants; here they used the wrong type of analysis'. When you can work out the strength of the evidence, you're in a better position to know which of the theories is the strongest, the most likely to be correct. Don't worry; I'll tell you specifically what to look for in the pages ahead.

The scientific method

The following sections explain each step of the scientific method and some of the issues involved with them. This is not a comprehensive coverage; I've cut it down to the minimum you need to know to get the largest initial benefit and you should continue your study using the books I recommend throughout.

There are many technical terms and issues involved in science and in research methods, and unfortunately they all have intimidating names. When your lecturers throw terms at you like 'independent variable', 'statistical significance', and 'unfalsifiability', it can be quite intimidating. It was for me, anyway.

What I have done with the following sections is describe each of these terms at the most relevant part of the scientific process, so you can see how everything fits into the overall process. I'll also give a few examples along the way which I hope will be memorable.

Take a few minutes to skim through all the steps before returning here to go through again in more depth.

The scientific cycle

One way of picturing science is as a cycle (see Figure 2.1), where theories about the world are continuously refined through systematic testing.

This whole process relies on having questions to ask – wanting to know something about reality that we don't already know or wanting to test something that we might be wrong about. There are many ways to come up with a question:

- by observing something in your life and wondering how or why it is like that
- by having knowledge of existing theories and identifying a direction for future research
- by noting that some previous experiments were of poor quality and deciding to replicate them in a more thorough way

. . . and so on.

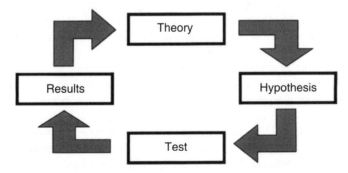

Figure 2.1 The scientific cycle

At any point in the cycle, a question can be devised. The cycle moves around, hypotheses are created, tested in experiments and the results of these tests are used to refine theories. Then a new hypothesis is created, tested and the cycle repeats continually. We'll look at each of these steps individually.

Theory

Science doesn't prove anything.

Journalists, TV presenters and advertisements often say that scientists have 'proven' something but this is never technically true and only adds to a general misunderstanding of science. There is no such thing as a scientific fact. All science can do is report what happened in an experiment, under the very specific conditions in which it was conducted.

Which, if you think about it logically, makes perfect sense. Here's a slightly extreme value of what this means. Right now I am typing this with one hand (somewhat slowly!) and in the other hand, I am holding your average office-variety pen. Science cannot say with 100 per cent certainty what will happen when I drop this pen. Let's try.

OK, it fell to the desk, just as you would predict. The key word here though, is predict. No scientist has ever been in this room at this exact time and conducted this experiment, so, in a very technical sense, no one fully knew what would happen. All we could do was make a prediction based on our existing knowledge and experiences with dropping things. Illusionists and magicians use this to their advantage when performing; their tricks violate our expectations and go against our existing knowledge of how the world works.

To put this another way, science is not able to verify claims, only to falsify them (or fail to do so); and failure to falsify a claim is not sufficient as affirmative proof. As Albert Einstein famously said: 'No amount of experimentation can ever prove me right; a single experiment can prove me wrong'.

Although it's impossible to test a theory in every possible situation, once we've tested a theory very thoroughly, we can be pretty sure we'll get the same results in future tests, as long as the conditions are not drastically different to the ones in our previous tests. Although no one has dropped the same pen in the same place at the same time as I did a moment ago, we all knew it would fall. Enough pens have been dropped that we knew what would happen. So, the more of these 'very specific conditions' in which the theory has been tested, the more likely that theory is to accurately reflect the objective world 'out there'. It's kind of like having more legs (tests) to support a table top (theory).

When a theory is strong – that is, supported by the results of many tests – we are able to make accurate predictions from it. Newton proposed his theory of gravitation in 1687, which he used to explain the orbits of the planets. Something that was of great interest to later scientists was Uranus (the planet, that is. I know what you're thinking).

When the movements of the planet Uranus could not be accounted for using the movements of the other planets, Newton's theory predicted that there was another planet up there. Later, Neptune was discovered, which provided strong support for Newton's theory.

This is how science progresses. Theoretical models of the world are made and scientists ask themselves: if this theory is correct, what else might be true? Then they go out and see if that particular 'what else' really is true. The results might support the theory or they might not, in which case the theory might have to be modified.

This potential for a theory to fail a test is an important aspect of science. A theory is only useful if it can be put 'on the line', just like Newton's theory. Had Neptune not existed, Newton's theory would have needed to be looked at again in light of this new evidence. Some theories cannot be placed 'on the line' in this way. For example, take the existence of a God. God is 'theorized' to be omnipotent and omnipresent. It's impossible to formulate a test that could disprove the existence of a God, because you can always say 'God made the experiment results turn out that way'. You might mention religious texts which explain what God does and does not do. But again you have the same problem: how do you test this without assuming something to begin with? Another example is psychic powers. If a psychic fails to demonstrate their psychic abilities in a controlled test, they can always say 'The sceptical vibes around me interfered with my powers'. There's an excellent character in the film *Mystery Men* who sums this up – his superhero power is the ability to turn invisible – but only when nobody is watching!

Maybe there is a God. Maybe there isn't. Maybe people are psychic. Maybe they aren't. The point is that these ideas cannot be tested; they are unfalsifiable. There is no conceivable way that they can be put on the line: there's always an 'out' that can be used to explain away negative results. In other words, it is impossible to find out whether the table top has legs. Science cannot be used to investigate topics that are unfalsifiable.

Special note on 'it's just a theory!'

I once watched a debate on whether creationism should be taught in science classes in public schools. There are only two TV shows that have actually made me throw my shoes at the TV screen and this was one of them (the other was that abomination, *Big Brother*). 'Today's topic', the presenter says: 'should creationism be taught in science classes in public schools?'.

Whack! Goes the first shoe. . .

One debater speaks up: 'Of course! Creationism is just as valid as any scientific theory!'

Smack! There goes the other one. . .

'You have to remember', he continues, 'evolution is just a theory!'

The TV is lucky I only have two feet!

'It's just a theory', is a common and nonsensical argument used against scientific theories by individuals who don't understand what a theory is (and they almost always start with 'You have to remember . . .' for some reason). The logic is that 'theory' must equal 'not fact' because this is how it is used in common vernacular: 'This should work in theory', 'She doesn't really know, she's an armchair theorist'. But in science, the word 'theory' is used whether the theory has 100 studies refuting it or 10,000 studies supporting it. Some theories are false, some are as close to being fact as science is able to give us. Don't get caught on the word 'theory'.

Hypothesis

Once a theory has been drawn up, scientists will go out and test the theory. To do this they create a hypothesis, which is a prediction about what might be true in the world, assuming the theory is correct, with the aim of testing these predictions against reality.

Suppose you have a theory proposing a number of physiological changes that occur through the practice of meditation. One of these is that some forms of meditation can increase body temperature. You wonder why this might be, since meditation is a relaxing state in which metabolism tends to lower. Your specific hypothesis, then, might be that this process works through vasodilation, rather than increased metabolism. If you tested this hypothesis, you might get results similar to Benson (1982), who recorded increased skin temperature during a form of 'heat' yoga but not increased rectal temperature (as measured by a 10cm probe – the things people do for science!).

The trick with hypotheses is to:

- make sure they really test the theory in question, and
- make them specific.

It's quite easy to come up with theories about the world but it's a bit tougher to think up testable hypotheses that represent a real way of testing those theories.

So, the hypothesis is the thing that is being predicted. In science, there is always one or more specific hypothesis. Studies are generally not conducted without making a prediction, just to 'see what happens,' with the exception of exploratory research. This is because, if you go out and collect a load of data, there are myriad ways you can cut it and slice it to make one point or another. Seriously, in any worthless data set you can probably find some fluke finding or other to report. If we built theories on results like this, they would be flimsy and poor predictors of the real world. Instead, we put our theories on the line – expose them to potential refutation. If they fail to be refuted over and over, we assume they are strong theories.

Because of this, pretty much all the statistical analyses that are done in science revolve around the fact that a hypothesis has been drawn up and is being tested. We'll come back to this point on page 29 when we talk about the null hypothesis.

Test

After we've examined or created a theory and drawn up a hypothesis, the next step in the scientific method is to design and carry out a study that will put our hypothesis to the test. As you'll see, this is not always as easy as it seems.

First of all let's briefly look at the two broad types of research methodologies that psychologists use when designing studies – quantitative and qualitative.

Quantitative methodologies include anything that involves numbers. How much? How many? Anything that is measured by being quantified or categorized, is quantitative. Pretty simple.

Qualitative methodologies cover any data in word form that isn't categorized, such as labels, descriptions, narratives, interview transcripts or diary entries.

Since psychology is very heavily biased towards quantitative methods, many students are relieved when they learn about qualitative methods, seeing them as a way to get out of statistics. This is flawed reasoning, because it is still necessary to understand statistical data to be able to read scientific papers properly. However, some people simply do have a greater affinity towards working with qualitative methods, which might involve reading through interview transcripts over and over to look for themes and patterns in what people have said (by the way, if you ever have to transcribe a number of interviews, find a transcription service online – it will save you hours of time and some are very cheap. If you can't find one, hire a freelancer at elance.com or fiverr.com).

Whether psychologists choose to use qualitative or quantitative research depends on many things. They might prefer one method or have more experience with it, the topic they are studying might lend itself more readily to one method rather than the other or perhaps a methodology hasn't yet been used in a given field and it's time to close that gap. Qualitative and quantitative methods come with their own advantages and disadvantages but quantitative is the more commonly used method by a long chalk. Let's take a closer look at this method and why it's used, then we'll come back to qualitative methods and compare the two approaches.

Variables

Quantitative studies revolve around defining and measuring variables. If a study has a variable, it is quantitative by definition. 'Variable' is simply the technical term for something that you are measuring or manipulating. For example:

- age
- weight
- gender
- happiness
- extraversion

. . . are all variables.

When designing a study, scientists have to decide what variables they are going to measure – which is determined by the hypothesis – and how they are going to measure them.

Sometimes the 'how' part is easy. Looking at the list above, the top two – age and weight – are easy to measure. We have well-known and established tools for doing so; namely, tape measures and weighing scales. The third is a little different. With gender, you have two categories: male and female, so it might be tempting to assume that this is a qualitative variable because it's not numerical – the categories 'male' and 'female' are qualitatively different; one isn't higher or lower than the other. However, non-numerical variables are still quantitative, they are just given a special name – categorical variables.

The next two, happiness and extraversion, are trickier. Unlike height, weight and gender, these are abstract constructs. You can't see them, you can't touch them and you could make a legitimate argument that they don't actually exist, that they're just things we talk about. However, a variable doesn't need to exist in this concrete sense for it to form part of a scientific theory. It's a *construct* – it's assumed to exist and if its addition to a scientific model helps to explain more data, it can stay in the model until something better comes along.

Whether the variable being studied is something concrete and physical or abstract and psychological, researchers still need to figure out accurate ways of quantifying and measuring that variable. This process is called *operationalization*.

Measuring variables

In psychology, many methods of measuring variables are used but most of them fall into one of three possibilities: what people say, what people do, and physical/biological measurements.

What people say

Perhaps the most common way of measuring variables in psychology is through *self-report* – in other words, what people say. Usually this is done through questionnaires which, rather than just asking any old question, are very carefully designed and tested. Typically, a questionnaire will present a series of statements to a participant and they will respond by stating how much they agree with it on a numerical scale, such as from one (strongly disagree) to seven (strongly agree). For example, a questionnaire measuring extraversion might ask people the extent to which they agree with statements like 'I go out to parties often' or 'I find it easier to strike up conversations with strangers'.

But here we have a problem. Although it is quicker and cheaper to ask someone how many parties they go to than it is to follow them around for a week and check for sure, there's always a chance that they won't give accurate answers. Maybe they don't want to seem boring, so they lie and say they've been to more parties than they actually have. Or maybe they get so drunk at parties that they're not sure how many they go to. This inaccuracy is a major downfall of self-report and perhaps a weakness of psychology overall, since this is the way that variables tend to be measured. Still, there are ways of increasing the accuracy of self-report questionnaires, which we'll discuss soon.

What people do

A second method is to observe people's behaviour under certain conditions. Vohs, Mead, & Goode (2006) primed people with images of money on a screensaver as they carried out a dummy task and had a researcher drop a box of pencils as a participant left the room. The number of pencils picked up by the participant was used as measure of prosocial behaviour, to see whether images of money reduced people's propensity to be helpful (it did). Examples of other behavioural measures include giving participants tasks to perform, quantifying their body language or simply making quantified observations on what they do.

Observing and measuring behaviour tends to be more expensive and time-consuming than giving out questionnaires but it is generally considered to be more accurate. Because it measures what participants actually do and not just what they say they will do, it is usually one step closer to the construct under study than self-report. However, there are exceptions, of course, and it's not always easy to tell whether a certain behaviour represents a certain psychological trait or not. People are generally quite aware of how their actions might lead them to be perceived so, just as with self-report, they may deliberately alter their behaviour to give a certain impression.

Physical measurements

These methods are also highly prized for their objectivity. Like behavioural measures, they sidestep the potential errors associated with self-report measures but they also tend to be more expensive. Their advantage lies in the fact that the participant has less control over the measurement. For example, imagine you're measuring people's stress levels. You could use a self-report scale but, as we've discussed, the participant might lie or give inaccurate responses. You might observe their body language but perhaps they are 'putting on a brave face' and appear less stressed than they actually are. So, instead, you might choose to measure cortisol levels, which gives you a biological marker of stress that is harder for the participant to influence. Other examples of physical measurements include:

- physiological markers like heart rate, galvanic skin response or muscle tension
- biological markers like immune response, hormone levels and the data provided by a suite of brain imaging.

Validity and reliability

Physical and behavioural measurements are more accurate but also more expensive and time-consuming. That's why self-report scales are more commonly used in psychology. However, psychologists don't just write any old set of questions and start handing surveys out. Instead, they refine their questions by testing them for *validity* and *reliability*. To explore these ideas, let's go back to the happiness example we looked at earlier.

We can assume that a number of behavioural and physiological measurements are related to happiness – for example, how much a person smiles, the activity in the left prefrontal cortex (a brain area related to positive emotion), whether their friends say they are happy, and so on.

To validate a self-report happiness questionnaire, you would take all these measurements in a group of people (or several groups) and also give them your questionnaire. If the results correlate positively – that is, if the people who gave high scores in the questionnaire also smiled more, had higher left prefrontal cortex activity, etc., you can be more confident that the questionnaire is accurate, that it measures the variable we're intending to measure. In other words, it has high *validity*.

As well as testing the validity of a measurement, it must also be tested for *reliability*. While validity gives you an idea of whether the instrument measures the construct it intends to measure, reliability tells you whether it gives stable measurements over time. A test retest procedure is used, where the same people are given the test at various intervals, such as after one week, one month and six months. Depending on the construct, you might expect greater or lesser reliability. For example, personality is often defined in psychology as traits that are stable over time. Thus, if your measure gives wildly different scores after six months, it's probably not measuring this construct. Likewise, if you measure mood on two occasions six months apart, you would expect there to be differences, because mood can vary from one day to the next, let alone six months apart.

Of course, no matter how well designed a self-report measure is, it cannot give you a completely accurate measurement. But nor can anything else. If you measure someone's height as 160cm, this isn't completely accurate. It might actually have been 160.125766cm at the time of measurement. However, 160cm is close enough for all intents and purposes. It's a similar scenario with self-report questionnaires. No matter how much time you spend developing and refining them by testing different questions, there will always be some measurement error. However, if, despite all this, the instrument passes your validation tests, you can still use it.

Summary

Let's go over the logic of operationalization again quickly. We:

- assume that a psychological construct exists
- try to measure it
- test the validity and reliability of our measurement method.

If it passes our validity and reliability checks, we continue to use this operational definition in the future. It doesn't matter if this construct physically exists or not, whether we can 'see' it – what matters is that we can measure it consistently. Going back to the happiness example, it doesn't matter whether there is a physical 'thing' called happiness. If we find a way to measure something and our validity tests indicate that it's similar to the lay idea of 'happiness', we can call it that. Or we might use a technical term instead. For example, psychologists often talk about 'subjective wellbeing', to show that they are talking about a very specific operational definition of happiness and not 'the' happiness – even assuming such a thing exists.

Sampling: getting people to take part in the study

Okay, so far so good. We've drawn a hypothesis from a theory, figured out what variables to measure and we know how to operationalize them. But of course, we also need to recruit some people to participate in the test. Sounds simple – but this is not as easy as going out into the street and grabbing the first 100 people we find.

Why not? People are people, so won't any group do? No, and the reason lies in the difference between *samples* and *populations*. A sample is simply a smaller number of people taken from a larger group, called a population. In an ideal world, the sample demographically represents the population very well. That is, if the population is the United States of America, you would hope that the sample used in the study does not differ from the country overall, on average, in the constructs you are investigating. In reality, this is hard to achieve. For example, imagine one of your variables is stress and you are taking your sample from a poor neighbourhood. Would your results generalize well to the country as a whole? Probably not. On the other hand, if you intend to generalize your results to other poor areas in the USA, you're probably in a better position to generalize.

Remember though, science can only tell us what happened in the very specific situations under which the study took place. So no one can say for sure whether the results of a study generalize to the larger population from which the sample came, no matter how well they match up. So we have two options. The first is to actually study the entire population. Of course, in most cases this is prohibitively expensive, especially if your population is the whole country or the human race! And even in the best attempts to do this, such as a government census, the results only apply to the specific *time* during which the data were collected. Even if you could run a perfect census and sample the whole population, every day people move home, get married, get divorced, die and give birth – so within hours the population has changed and the data no longer represent it! So we're left with the second option – recruit the best sample we can and hope for the best.

What is the 'best' sample? The standard to aim for is called the *simple random sample*. This means that every person in the target population has an equal chance of ending up in your sample. The idea is that, if you use a large enough sample and it's randomly selected, the average measurement of the variables you're studying will be the same or at least very similar. One way to do this is to put the name of everyone in your population into a computer and have it randomly select your sample for you. However, this ideal scenario almost never happens, mainly owing to cost and logistical difficulties. Therefore, a more common scenario is to use an *opportunity sample*; that is, whoever is easiest to recruit at the time of recruiting.

Unless you haven't started your course yet, you'll have noticed that you are required to take part in a few psychology studies as a participant yourself if you want to pass. This is a prime example of opportunity sampling and, as you read more and more research papers, you'll become very familiar with the participants section saying something like 'Participants were 86 undergraduate students who took part for course credit'. This is rife in psychology and it's a huge criticism that can be made of the field. A great deal of research is conducted on psychology students with the assumption that the results generalize to other demographics but is that the case? Psychology students are predominantly female, tend to be 18–21, within a certain socioeconomic bracket, perhaps of a certain IQ, and so on.

Does that mean that any study lacking a simple random sample is worthless? No, but it does mean that more care must be taken when generalizing the results to people outside that sample.

Hey, you psychology students are free and available and you can be forced to take part in studies at little cost to the university. So why not use you? It's better to have those data than not have them. And of course, some things are more generalizable than others – research on perceptual systems perhaps, which probably operate similarly in psychology students as they do in any other adult population. Just make sure that, when conducting studies, you try to be as unbiased as you can and, when reading studies, you take a moment to note who the sample is and who they might generalize to (or not).

OK, now that we have our participants, it's time to run the test.

The experimental method

The experimental design is a research methodology used in psychology to look for cause-and-effect relationships between variables. It's not the only research design used but it is the best one for this particular purpose. Once you understand the logic of the experiment, it will be easier to understand other methods and their relative strengths and weaknesses; so we'll start here and then look at some different methods afterwards.

An experiment is not just a general term used to describe any old test. The general idea of an experiment is to manipulate a particular variable while keeping other variables constant, then observe the effect this has on something else. What does it mean to hold other variables constant? Here's an example. I've heard that if you think you might be allergic to a certain food, the best thing to do is to remove things from your diet one at a time for a few weeks. If your symptoms clear up, you've found a good contender for the offending food group. If you cut out dairy, grains, processed meats and fruit all at the same time and then your symptoms clear up, how would you know which of the four you're allergic to? You wouldn't be able to tell. That's why you need to test them one at a time while keeping everything else constant. So you're keeping the other variables (other food groups) constant (eating them as normal) while you manipulate (stop eating) another.

The rules of the experimental method work on this principle: isolating, as much as possible, a single variable, manipulating it, then measuring another variable to see if it also changes. Ahead, we'll look at the main issues involved in experiments but first let's define some terms.

The independent variable and the dependant variable

In an experiment (as in other types of research), special terms are given to the variable we are manipulating and the variable we are observing. The variable that the experimenter *manipulates* in the study is the *independent variable* or IV for short. The variable being measured is the *dependent variable* or DV. Here's an example.

I have previously mentioned my strong urge to throw my shoes at the TV whenever reality TV programmes come on. That's a good idea for a study: 'The impact of reality TV shows on the desire to throw footwear'. To do this, I'll recruit a sample and split them into two groups. One group will watch some reality TV, while the other, a control group, will watch something else, a wildlife documentary or maybe just a blank screen. I'll put a few reasonably aerodynamic shoes near the participants and measure how many were thrown over the course of the shows.

What is the IV in this case? What am I manipulating? I'm manipulating what people watch on the TV. One group watches reality TV, the other doesn't, so I'm manipulating the participants' viewing experience from one group compared with the next.

What is the DV? What am I measuring? It's the number of shoes thrown. This, I hypothesise, is *dependent* on what people watch on TV. Remember it like this:

The dependent variable is dependent on the independent variable.

Control groups and random assignment

In the above example, why do we need to include a control group? Can't we just sit people at the TV watching *Big Brother* and count how many shoes they throw? Nope, and in fact, any experiment that does not use a suitable control group is flawed. I'll use some more realistic examples to explain.

Say we're testing the effect of a new drug on symptoms of depression. Our problem as researchers is making sure that any results we collect are due to an effect of the medication and nothing else – as closely as we can. This is difficult for us, because many things can improve depression besides our drug: spontaneous improvement, the placebo effect or the attention from the researchers when giving the pills out, to name a few. So to isolate the IV we need to do a *controlled trial*; we use two groups, which we try to match as closely as possible except for one thing – the IV; whether they get the drug or a sugar pill. Both groups are equally liable to the placebo and other effects, so if our drug group ends up with lower symptoms, we can have more confidence that the improvement is caused by the drug itself.

However, if you were an unscrupulous pharmaceutical company and wanted to make your drug look good even though it isn't, you could manipulate this system to your advantage. You could take all the people who look like they are on the road to recovery and put them in the treatment group, then put all the hopeless cases in your control group. This way, all you have to do is keep the study going long enough and, hey presto, a positive result you can use to sell your drug. Of course, this is highly unethical and bad scientific practice, so researchers will try to assign participants to groups *randomly*.

Random group assignment is the fairest way to remove bias when allocating participants to groups. You might think that trying to match the two groups as closely as possible would be fairest but it isn't. For one thing, until human cloning is brought into psychological research, you will never match groups perfectly and, for another, there's always that temptation – perhaps unconscious – to allocate participants in ways that might be favourable to your desired outcome. The idea is that – assuming your sample is large enough and is as close to a simple random sample as possible – random assignment will bring you very well-matched groups in any case. That is to say, if you have two groups of 100 people each, they are likely to have the same average height, the same average extraversion, the same average

IQ, the same average happiness and so on. This is just because human traits tend to be distributed among populations in predictable ways.

So how do we randomize groups? The answer is, the closer the method is to being 'truly' random, the better. A computer algorithm is not truly random but it's pretty good. Manual methods can also be used, such as a dice roll or a coin toss, but the more manual the method, the more open it is to interference from the researcher. With a dice roll, for instance, there's always that little possibility of 'Oh it landed on its side . . . better re-roll!' The best way is to use a true random number generator, such as the one at random.org, which you can use for free.

Experimental control

As I explained earlier, in science you are usually trying to isolate the effect of one variable, so you try to control as many other variables as you possibly can. While controlling these other variables does indeed help us to do this, it comes at a cost. Here's another example.

Why do we find ourselves getting hot for certain people and turned off by others? An evolutionary theory to explain this is that we have systems in our brain that respond to people who might be good mates and provide us with healthy children. To this end, it is thought that women prefer indicators of status and men are more attracted to physical characteristics. Gueguen (2007) tested this theory, investigating whether breast size had a role to play in male attraction. To do this, he conducted a test in a few nightclubs, to see if women with larger breasts would be approached more often by men.

Let's fill in the blanks of this study design based on what we've covered so far. The theory is the idea that male mate selection is influenced by the physical characteristics of females. The researcher did a literature search and found that breast size may be associated with attraction in males. From this, his hypothesis was that males will make more approaches to women with larger breasts in nightclubs.

Think about how you might conduct this study. Would you take five women with different breast sizes and put them in five different nightclubs to see how often they are approached? Well, you could do this but how would you know whether it was their breasts and not, say, their hairstyle, that attracted the man? Remember, nothing is assumed and everything is tested.

Of course, hairstyle is not the only thing that might contaminate the results. Other problematic variables might be the body shape of the woman, her height, what she was wearing, the atmosphere of each nightclub, the music that it plays, the clientele it attracts. All these annoying things that get in the way of knowing whether breast size is what is really attracting the males are called *extraneous variables*. Extraneous variables are nuisances. The more of them there are, and the stronger their presence is, the further our study moves from being a true test of our hypothesis. They prevent us from properly testing our theories and, hence, keep us from the truth.

So, to get around these problems, the experimenter used the same woman, took her to 12 different nightclubs and instructed her to wear the same clothes each time. The only difference was padding in her bra from the 'A' of her natural size to the 'B' and 'C' of the experimental conditions, that were chosen at random each night.

This is an example of how extraneous variables can be controlled – by using the same person, variables like facial attractiveness, clothing, hair colour and so on are kept constant. But it is impossible to control for everything. By conducting 12 tests, many variables, like her mood, body language or the confidence of men out each night might be averaged out. Another issue is that maybe she felt more attractive or more confident when wearing the padded bra. It's conceivable that this added confidence was attracting the men, rather than the breast size itself. This is a special type of extraneous variable, called a *confounding variable* or *confounding factor* – it varies *with* the independent variable. It's hard to separate an effect caused by a change in the IV from an effect caused by a change in the confounding factor, because they change together – they correlate.

Given all the problems mentioned above, is it best to control for as many extraneous variables as we possibly can?

Ecological validity: controlling your way from reality

It's not just confidence that we have to control for. Maybe the woman's facial expressions were different each night. Maybe her posture was slightly different. What if the song that was playing made a difference to whether men approached her? So many extraneous variables! To totally control for all these things, what could we do? Put her in a white room and inject her with some drug to give her temporary paralysis? Or maybe we could take photographs of her and manipulate the IV with Adobe Photoshop and then ask people to rate these pictures for attractiveness?

We could do this and we would certainly control for many variables. But the more of these variables we control for, the further our study gets from the real world in which we live. Distance from reality, in a way, is an extraneous variable in itself. This is known as *ecological validity*. If you have made the conditions of your study so specific that people do not behave the same way when they are not in these conditions, there is little point to your experiment. Your theory refers to the real world but your experiment was conducted somewhere else. So you can only provide minimal support for your theory – if any. This is *low ecological validity*.

The other end of the scale is to do a naturalistic observation – get out in nightclubs with a clipboard and count up who approaches who. Because you're not interfering or controlling anything, this has *high ecological validity*. Unfortunately, the closer you get to reality, the less control you have and so the more extraneous variables there are to get in the way of testing your hypothesis! What is the best way: more control or higher ecological validity?

Both. Researchers conduct experiments under a variety of conditions, using different methodologies. They might do some studies under highly controlled conditions, some under more naturalistic settings (i.e., real world observations) and some that are in between (like the nightclub experiment, for instance). We hope that all of this evidence will point in the same direction and support the theory. This is called *converging evidence*. A scientist's work is never done.

Blinding

I hope that the previous sections have given you an idea of why control is necessary in experiments – particularly the use of a control group – there are many things that might affect your results besides your IV; randomly assigning participants to the experimental group or the control group helps to control for these things. Perhaps the most important of these is the placebo effect. Sometimes, if people believe they are receiving a powerful drug, even if they are actually only receiving a placebo – that is, a sugar pill with no active ingredients in it – their body reacts as if they had been given the actual drug. The power of their belief causes the effect.

This applies to other types of treatments and interventions too; new counselling methods, sports psychology techniques, new educational methods – all are susceptible to the placebo effect. If a clinical psychologist tells a patient to try a certain exercise and it works, was it the exercise that brought the effect or was it simply being told to do something by a friendly person with letters after their name that brought the benefits?

When testing a treatment, it's really important to find a way around this placebo problem and the solution is *blinding*. You still randomly allocate your participants to the two groups – the treatment group and the control group – but you don't tell them which group they are in. This is a *single-blind trial*. Both groups are susceptible to the placebo effect, therefore it's controlled for, it is held constant across the groups. This way, the drug being studied has to cause an effect over and above the placebo effect.

However, single-blinding, while better than no blinding at all, is actually flawed. Imagine that you really, really want your new drug to work. When you are talking to your participants and giving them the pills they'll be taking for the period of the test, you unconsciously behave more kindly and optimistically to your treatment group. Even if you don't actually say that they are getting the real drug, your optimism might rub off on them and cause a placebo effect. Luckily, there's a step you can take to prevent this, which is to make the study *double-blind*. In a double-blind trial, the person administering the drug or treatment does not get to know which participants are getting the real drugs. Perhaps a second researcher performs the group allocation and puts the names on the pill bottles; you don't find out until after the study is complete. Another way of double-blinding is to test an intervention without one-to-one contact with the participant. The study might be conducted online using written instructions, taking care that they are phrased as closely as possible between groups. This means that the researcher's influence on the participants is held perfectly constant between groups, because they all get the same instructions.

In psychology it's a little harder to come up with placebo equivalents to fake tablets but it can be done. They might take the form of dummy exercises and activities that take the same amount of time and effort but are unlikely to have any direct effect on the DV. For example, if you're testing the effects of writing about traumatic events on post-traumatic stress disorder, a control exercise could be writing about what happened today. This helps to draw out the effects of writing about your trauma from the effects of being told to write something by an authority figure.

Double-blinding is sometimes harder to achieve in psychology, though, and in many cases it's simply not possible. Imagine you wanted to test an alternative therapy like Reiki on depression. Reiki involves hovering the hands over, but not touching, the participant's body and healing their woes through some alleged energetic process. Here's something that is wide open to the placebo effect; so it's necessary to blind the test. However, while it is possible to single-blind this test – that is, leave the participants in the dark as to whether the therapist is really doing Reiki above their back or just making shadow puppets – you can't double-blind it. The therapist knows whether they are actually doing Reiki or not. In situations like this you just have to make do with single-blinding.

Replication

All of the above rules and regulations of the experimental method are safeguards, helping scientists to be as sure as possible that their experiment is a fair test of their hypothesis. But, no matter how well a test is conducted, a single study is not enough. The test needs to be repeated, preferably many times over, by different scientists in different labs. This process is called *replication*.

Scientists replicate experiments for a number of reasons. There might be something they missed in the methodology, perhaps something they failed to control for. They might be unconsciously influencing the results in some way. But even if a test is performed flawlessly, there's still the possibility of getting a particular outcome just by chance. As a field, psychology is particularly susceptible to this because it deals with those pesky unpredictable humans. Say you're testing a new psychological intervention on anxiety but, unbeknownst to you, it's a bogus therapy. It doesn't work. You run your test perfectly – you use large sample sizes, double-blinding, random group assignment and you control for all the extraneous variables. Your test was perfect. However, by pure unprecedented fluke, everyone in your treatment group spontaneously improves. It had nothing to do with your test, they just got better. Your results would be consistent with the conclusion that the intervention worked – even though it didn't!

The point of replication is that a single study is not enough to back up a hypothesis – even when it's fantastically conducted. The study needs to be replicated numerous times. Psychology is well-known for its lack of replication – always keep an eye out for this when reading papers: has the experiment been replicated? What were the results?

Types of test

The randomized controlled trial just described is called a *true experiment* and, for the reasons we've just discussed, it has the best chance of coming to a firm cause-and-effect conclusion. In fact, it is the *only* method capable of doing so. However, it is not always possible to conduct a true experiment, even if you want to. For example, imagine you want to compare males against females on some variable – you cannot randomly assign people to a gender! So it might be useful at this point to go over a few other types of test available and why they are used. You should make it a goal to be able to recognize which of these categories any journal paper fits into.

Quasi-experiment

A quasi-experiment is similar to a true experiment, except that it doesn't quite tick all the boxes necessary for it to be labelled as such. Any experiment which does not directly manipulate the IV – for example by not performing random group assignment – is a quasi-experiment. You might test males against females, a high-income group against a low-income group, or you may have already collected the data for a treatment group and then subsequently recruit and study a control group. Quasi-experiments cannot tell us about cause and effect with full certainty, because a potential effect of the IV on the DV cannot be distinguished from an effect of the group assignment procedure on the DV.

Non-experimental designs

Sometimes we just want to observe people and see what they do, without taking any active steps to manipulate an IV. Here, we are the furthest away from making a cause-and-effect conclusion because, since we're not intervening in any way, we can't separate the variable we're observing from anything else. There are a three common study designs that fall into this category: longitudinal, naturalistic observation and cross-sectional.

A *longitudinal design* is one in which a group of participants is followed over time, sometimes many years, and certain variables are tracked. It is useful in cases where the variable of interest cannot be manipulated for ethical reasons, for instance, when studying the effect of a potentially harmful drug. Although useful, we cannot determine cause and effect from this design, as we're not manipulating the independent variable. Sometimes a group will be compared over time with a matched control group, which is demographically similar. This is like combining a longitudinal study with a quasi-experiment but, because there was no random assignment and no IV manipulation, it is still not an experiment.

A *naturalistic observation* is simply where participants are observed in some natural setting and measurements are taken. Although you might get an image of a field researcher hiding in public with a clipboard and binoculars, this broad type of study can take other forms, for example using global positioning service data in smartphones to study people's movements (with consenting participants, of course).

A *cross-sectional* design involves collecting data from each participant only once and assessing the relationships within those data. This is often called *correlational* data, for reasons that will become clear in the next chapter. This design includes survey and questionnaire studies, interviews and all of the qualitative methods, as well as literal observation studies. Cause and effect cannot be determined from a cross-sectional study, where data were collected on only one occasion and no IV manipulation took place.

Case studies and the problem with anecdote

Since a randomized, controlled, double-blind trial is the best method we know of to determine cause and effect, you'd expect it to crop up more often in marketing campaigns. Yet, instead, the most common method seems to be a testimonial from a happy customer. You've no doubt seen these in magazines, 'infomercials', billboards and pretty much anywhere else you care to look. There'll be a quote from 'Bob' from Tennessee, who loves Acme facial scrub more than life itself. Related to testimonials are anecdotes; my personal favourite anecdote is the 'I know a person who . . .' comment. 'I know a person who smoked all their life and didn't get lung cancer, therefore it can't be true.' 'I know a person whose psoriasis was cured by homeopathy.' 'I know a person who . . . whatever.'

Based on what you've read so far, why does science opt for expensive and time-consuming experiments over case studies and anecdotes as evidence? Let's look at just a few reasons:

- *Selection bias* – Case studies are not randomly selected from the population, that's for sure. No matter what your product or claim is – whether it's some alternative remedy, special beauty cream or psychic power – you can always find some people who swear that it works for them. And maybe it does work – for them – but how do we know they're not the only person it works for?
- *The placebo effect* – If you tell enough people that a jar of coloured water will heal them, some will be healed through the power of their own belief.
- *Belief bias* – the human mind is programmed to give greater weight to arguments that agree with currently existing beliefs; we're not objective.
- *They only look at one side of the story* – How many people smoked all their life and did develop lung cancer? What's the ratio?

Anecdotes can be used to give the appearance of support for an idea or the appearance of refutation of an existing example. In the former case, now that you've seen how careful scientists have to be about checking and double-checking every little fact, you can see how ridiculous it is to cherry-pick a few case studies and call it evidence. It's not evidence. It's marketing. And it doesn't matter how many case studies are used either, because they could all be cherry-picked. Remember this:

The plural of anecdote is not data.

Qualitative research

Let's return now to the qualitative methods I introduced briefly at the start of this chapter. Despite the growing popularity of qualitative methods, most of psychology is focused around the quantitative approaches that we've just discussed. There are many advantages to this. Quantitative studies are often – though not always – a cheaper, quicker and more objective approach than qualitative research. They allow you to measure variables, determine cause and effect, put you in a better position to generalize your results to larger populations and let you to make better comparisons between groups of data. Plus, certain things only make sense quantitatively, like height, weight, age, etc. Remember the study I mentioned about the meditators and their rectal thermometers? Imagine if that study was carried out qualitatively. What would you do, interview the participants and ask them if the temperature of their skin is higher then, *ahem*, elsewhere? It doesn't make sense to do that qualitatively.

This works both ways, however, and there are many instances where the quantitative method comes up short. Imagine using quantitative data to collect information on how people attempt to cope with a terminal illness. You might ask: on a scale of one-to-seven, how often do you feel stressed? How much do you reach out to others for support? and so on. But by only giving the participant the option to tell you about certain things which you decide in advance, you are forcing the results to go in a certain direction. You'll never capture the full story.

Therefore, the qualitative approach is more exploratory in nature. It holds fewer assumptions about what it expects to find and therefore provides a wider lens from which to look at the human condition. For this reason, qualitative is usually described as providing 'richer' data than quantitative. This makes it more suitable for investigating the subjective portion of the human life – you can get a more accurate idea of what a person's experience was actually like in a certain situation.

Although there is much criticism of the alternative method by strong proponents in both camps, both approaches can be used in a given field of research. Qualitative methods can be used to get the wider, richer snapshot that they are capable of obtaining, which can then be used to generate hypotheses about the phenomenon at hand. These hypotheses can then be studied with the narrow focus provided by quantitative methods. For example, if rates of teenage pregnancy were on the rise and you had been hired by your government to find out how to lower them, you might start with some exploratory qualitative work. You could interview teenagers and ask them about their experience, how they ended up pregnant, if they were happy about that, if it was an accident or a conscious choice, and so on. Perhaps the cause is not recklessness or lack of access to contraceptives; maybe it's something else. Qualitative methods can give you some ideas on that. Then you can devise an intervention programme and use quantitative methods to measure its effect.

The qualitative/quantitative debate is raging fiercely at the moment and it is likely to continue in the future. If you find that you fall strongly on one side of the fence, don't neglect the other – learn about both methods in depth and understand their relative strengths and weaknesses. Above all, don't allow your preferences to solidify your thinking or make you confrontational with people from 'the other side.'

Results

The next step in the scientific method is the analysis and interpretation of the results. The previous steps exist to give us accurate results and, as you have seen, this takes a lot of effort. Once the data have been collected, they will be analyzed. There is a full section on the analysis of test results in the next chapter so I won't go into that here. After the analysis, researchers discuss whether the results support the hypothesis and what the implications are for the theory from which the hypothesis was drawn.

Peer review

A full report of the test is created giving information on the entire process I have just described. The researchers explain how they devised their hypothesis, give a detailed description of how they carried out the test and an in-depth discussion of how their data affect present theories (if at all). This paper is sent to a journal, where the editor has a look and decides if it's any good. The editor has the option here to reject it, perhaps because it's not suitable for the subject of the journal or that it is simply a flawed study. If the paper passes the editor's first review, it is sent out for *peer review*. Experts in the same field as the paper's topic receive a copy and they give feedback to the editor on the quality of the paper. They grade the paper in on of three ways: publishable quality as it stands, publishable after a few changes have been made or not publishable. If changes are needed, the researchers get the paper back, along with the feedback, make the amendments and then resubmit the paper.

There are many advantages to this method of publishing. The main one is to ensure that the quality of published research is high. The reviewers are typically highly experienced in their field and are able to point out obvious flaws or methodological errors that would call the results into question. Note that the reviewers are not supposed to approve or reject papers just because they don't agree with the conclusions but, rather, to ensure that the quality of the science is high, that the test was well-conducted.

Peer review is an important part of the dissemination of scientific literature but it is not perfect. Editors and reviewers are only human and they are subject to bias just like the rest of us – consciously or unconsciously. For example, if the editor disagrees with a paper or dislikes the author, they might send it to reviewers who are known to be more nit-picky, in the hope that they will reject it. Also, in some cases, the author of the paper is able to suggest which reviewer the paper should be sent to. This is ostensibly because as they are familiar with their own speciality, they know who is best able to judge the quality of their work. However, if one of their old friends or colleagues is a reviewer for that journal, they could try to get their work in front of that person, who might be more lenient. To counteract instances of bias like this, sometimes the reviewer won't be told who the authors of the paper are – however, this is not a very effective measure because it would be fairly simple for a reviewer to work out who the author of a paper is.

Thus, although it's not a perfect system, peer review is a very useful quality control procedure, which helps to keep lower-quality work from influencing scientific theories.

Back to theory

If the study was well conducted and controlled, and challenges the present theory, the theory will be modified in light of this new evidence – although usually not until after the results have been replicated. This is what stands science apart from other disciplines of knowledge – theories change in light of new evidence, as opposed to evidence being creatively interpreted to fit existing theories.

This does seem like a lot of work, doesn't it? The whole process from identifying a problem, designing and carrying out a study, and publishing the results, usually takes years. That's the major disadvantage of science – it is slow. However, speed is not the concern; accuracy is. People have the propensity get things wrong and to lie to themselves (and others); that's why science needs all these complicated rules and procedures. If someone wants to use science to lie, it will be difficult and costly for them to do and it will be possible for other researchers to scrutinise the lie and expose it.

The point of science is to arrive at results that we're as sure as we can be are accurate. These observations are then used to inform our theories. Unfortunately, despite all these safeguards, it is still possible for incorrect observations to slip through the net, either through error or design. Look into the track record of the pharmaceutical industry for some creative examples of this.

Further reading

This chapter is a broad overview of the scientific method and some of the problems associated with getting accurate information about the world. But it's just an overview; to deepen your knowledge, see the following:

- *How to think straight about psychology* by Keith E. Stanovich
  Every psychology student should read this. In explaining the scientific method, critical reasoning, and how they apply to psychology, this book is simply the best.
- *Bad Science* by Ben Goldacre
  Goldacre has practically made a career out of debunking 'bad science' – wherever you find homoeopaths, beauty creams or nutritionists, you'll find Ben turning his critical eye to their antics. This book is very accessible and explains a lot of concepts that are essential to a psychology degree.

3   Statistics and analysis

Everything we looked at in the previous chapter is vitally important if psychologists want to get closer to 'the truth'. A study needs to build on, challenge, develop or otherwise supplement the existing knowledge base by testing a carefully crafted hypothesis. The design of the study should help researchers move towards a solid understanding of the cause-and-effect relationships of what they want to study and care should be taken to ensure that they are measuring what they think they are measuring, without extraneous variables and researcher bias getting in the way.

But all of that effort is for nothing if the data are not analyzed correctly. Unless appropriate statistical techniques are used – and used properly – it does not matter how well the study was designed and conducted. The results are meaningless.

I imagine that statistics is the part of your psychology course that you enjoy the least. I remember most people hated it when I did my degree. Contrary to popular belief, this is actually a good thing. The reason is that the work you submit is not typically marked in absolute terms; rather, you and your classmates are marked off against each other. Of course, some work is simply good and other work simply not so good but if you had a class full of geniuses, it's unlikely they would all get top marks. Marking is relative.

So think about it. If most people in your classes hate statistics, are they likely to be good at it? Nope. They might have a basic grasp but they will make mistakes and they will lose marks that you will pick up.

So even though you might not like it (at first), and it feels far too much like hard work, learn statistics and analysis inside and out. You should know, by heart, the following things for each of the main statistical procedures:

- when it should be used
- how to read test results as written in the journals
- what the test is able to tell you and what it is not.

Don't be intimidated by the statistical side of psychology. You're probably only scared of it because:

- it's new to you
- there is a lot of intimidating terminology
- you set high standards for yourself
- you've identified yourself as a person who is 'bad with numbers' and are unwilling to change that identity.

The last point is the most important. Most people who say things like 'I'm rubbish with statistics', or 'I don't understand numbers' have not spent a long time learning it because they are so sure that they are 'bad with stats,' they don't even try.

In my first year at university, most people went to the three-hour research methods lecture each week but the only additional study they did was for the assignments and exams. I know, because I was one of them (which is probably why I failed research methods in year 1). I would not expect to learn a new language by listening to someone speak in it for three hours and then forgetting about it for the rest of the week. Statistics is simply the language psychologists have chosen to describe their data.

Take it slowly and use the study skills described later in the book to make it easier for yourself. Learn a little each day, focus on the task at hand when you are studying, give it your full attention and, when there are specific areas that you don't understand, go visit one of your lecturers (see page 78 for how to get more information out of your lecturers without being seen as a nuisance). Don't fear it! No one is terrible with statistics; there are just people who have learned and people who haven't.

In fact, regardless of your starting point, I recommend that you take an advanced research methods module, if there is one available to you. For one thing, the knowledge you gain from that will enhance all your other classes (not to mention your dissertation), giving a better return on the effort you put in than most modules but, also, research methods assessment tends to be a little easier, at least in the UK. There are definite right/wrong answers, you don't need to write creative criticisms of complex theories and you might get multiple choice rather than essay exams.

Before we get started, let me first point out that this chapter is definitely not exhaustive when it comes to stats information. Rather than the finer points of how the tests work, I'll just tell you what the tests do and how to interpret them. My aim is simply to give you:

- the broad, birds-eye view of the types of analyses that psychologists do, so that you'll understand the questions that they are asking when they do these tests
- enough information that you will be able to read most journal papers
- a reference guide that you can refer to quickly when reading papers, rather than search through a 600+ page textbook because you've forgotten what something means.

If you already have a good grasp of this topic, you can skip these chapters if you like. If not, let's continue.

Four common statistical procedures

Most analyses done by psychologists can be put into one of two categories, with each one having two very commonly used tests. There are a few exceptions but, usually, psychologists either want to know what the *relationship* is between two (or more) variables (i.e., do they correlate?) or they want to know whether two (or more) sets of data are *different* from each other and to what extent.

Relationships

An example of a time that researchers would investigate the relationship between two variables is the correlation between income levels and happiness, which I mentioned earlier. Do people with higher incomes also tend to also be happier and people with low incomes less happy? Or do you get happy and unhappy people at all income levels? The two most common tests to answer these types of questions are:

- correlation
- regression.

Differences

An example of a time when researchers might want to look for differences between sets of data would be in the trial of a new drug, to compare the results of the group given the drug with the results of the placebo control group. The two most common tests to answer these questions are:

- t test
- analysis of variance (ANOVA).

All four tests fall into a category called *parametric tests* and most of the other tests you will come across in journal papers are simply variations on these ones. In fact, these four are actually very similar to each other. So, although all the different statistical methods might seem varied and complicated, if you understand these two main themes, you'll have a better understanding of data analysis in general.

The null hypothesis

In science, statistical analyses are typically used to test hypotheses. We came across the hypothesis back on page 10. When you test a hypothesis, you are testing the possibility that your hypothesis is correct against the possibility that it isn't. The latter possibility is the null hypothesis – a prediction that the variables are not related (or not different) in the real world. For example, if your hypothesis is that people with a higher income have less stress, the null hypothesis is that income has no correlation with stress. If your hypothesis is that blondes have more fun, what's the null hypothesis? Is it:

d analysis

less fun

s not related to amount of fun?

t's not (a), because that is a hypothesis in itself, a prediction of an effect
(b) does not predict an effect – it's the prediction that there is no effect,
~~~ng blonde has no relationship with the amount of fun one has.

Remember earlier when we talked about science not proving anything? This is reflected in null-hypothesis testing. You see, one problem we might have in a study is getting results that support our hypothesis even though our hypothesis is not correct in the real world. It's possible that our impressive results might have been a complete fluke and there is always a certain probability of this. Our aim, then, is not to prove that the hypothesis is correct but to demonstrate that there is only a small probability that we would have got these results by chance if our hypothesis were actually incorrect. If that chance is suitably small, we can reject the null hypothesis.

An example might help to explain the philosophy of null-hypothesis testing. Say I create a loaded die that I believe will always roll a six. I've invited you round to my house tonight for a nice cup of tea and a spot of gambling. I plan to hustle you out of lots of money (don't worry, we're good friends and always playing tricks like this on each other). Of course, before you arrive I want to test my hypothesis that this die is loaded and always rolls a six against my null hypothesis that the die rolls will be random, like a normal die. I roll the die. Success! A six. But wait, there's actually a one-in-six chance that I would have gotten this result, even if the null hypothesis was correct. Not good enough. Better roll again. Another six! That's more like it; there's only a one-in-thirty-six chance of getting two sixes, assuming the null hypothesis is correct.

I could keep rolling – and the more sixes I rolled, the lower the probability that my results are down to chance and the more confident I can be about rejecting the null hypothesis. Whenever you see an analysis in a journal paper, you will also be given the probability that those results, or greater, would have come about by chance, assuming that the null hypothesis is true. It's given as p. So with a t test, for example, you would see something like this:

$$t = 3.52, p = .01$$

The statistic p is always between 0 and 1. Zero means 0 per cent chance of getting these results, assuming that the null hypothesis is true; 1 means 100 per cent chance, .5 means 50 per cent, and so on. Here, there is a 1 per cent chance we got this t of 3.52 by chance.

The next question is: what value of p do we look for to be confident enough to reject the null? In my gambling example, I stopped testing after two rolls of the die; 1:36, which calculates to around 2.7 per cent chance. So my p value is $p = .027$. We have to put the cut-off point somewhere. Is .027 good enough?

It is good enough for psychologists, who look for p values below $p = .05$, or 5 per cent. That's roughly the chance of rolling a double-six on two attempts. If the p value is lower than .05, the result is said to be statistically significant. To put this in perspective, if you do 20 tests and get p = .05 for each of them, it's odds-on that, in one of them, the results are down to chance and not the thing you're studying. Now think about how many thousands of psychology papers have been published over the decades! Earlier on, we talked about the need to replicate studies – here's another good reason to do so – if you do enough studies in your career, you'll get some positive results by fluke.

We would call this a type-I error – assuming an effect where there isn't really an effect. So, should we look for lower p values then? We could do. We could set the cut-off point (also called the alpha) to something like .01, or .001. But then we're in danger of making a type-II error – assuming there is no effect when really there is one. The .05 value is merely a guideline, a reasonable figure that isn't too hard to achieve and at the same time hard enough to stop some type-I errors slipping through the net.

So when you 'are looking at a research paper, check the p value of the tests. If it's .001, the result would seem very solid. If it's .048, it is barely significant and relatively a more questionable study. One thing to note here is that the way p is calculated takes into account the number of participants in the analysis. If you do two tests, one with 10 participants and one with 10,000, the latter test will have a lower p value, even if the results were the same. This is useful at low sample sizes because it means that you are less likely to make strong inferences on small amounts of data but it can cause problems in huge studies because no matter how small the effect, the results are likely to come out significant.

Statistical significance is a useful guideline but, just because a test is statistically significant doesn't mean it is *psychologically* significant. You have to look at the overall story that the paper is telling. With that out of the way, let's move on to the individual tests.

Correlation

With a correlation you are looking for the relationship between two variables (always two). There are three possible relationships:

- *Positive correlation*: when one variable is high, the other one is high. There is a positive correlation between height and weight. Tall people tend to weigh more than short people. If you know someone is taller than average, there's a fair chance they are also heavier than average.
- *Negative correlation:* when one variable is high, the other one is low. There is a negative correlation between temperature and the amount of clothes people wear. When the temperature is high, the amount of clothes people wear is low. When the temperature is low, the amount of clothing is high.
- *No correlation:* there is no relationship between two variables. When there is no correlation, there is no relationship; when one is high, the other might be high or low. I remember one study that rather surprisingly found no correlation between IQ and net wealth. Intelligent people can be wealthy or poor and so can blockheads. According to that study, knowing someone's IQ alone does not mean you can predict their income any better.

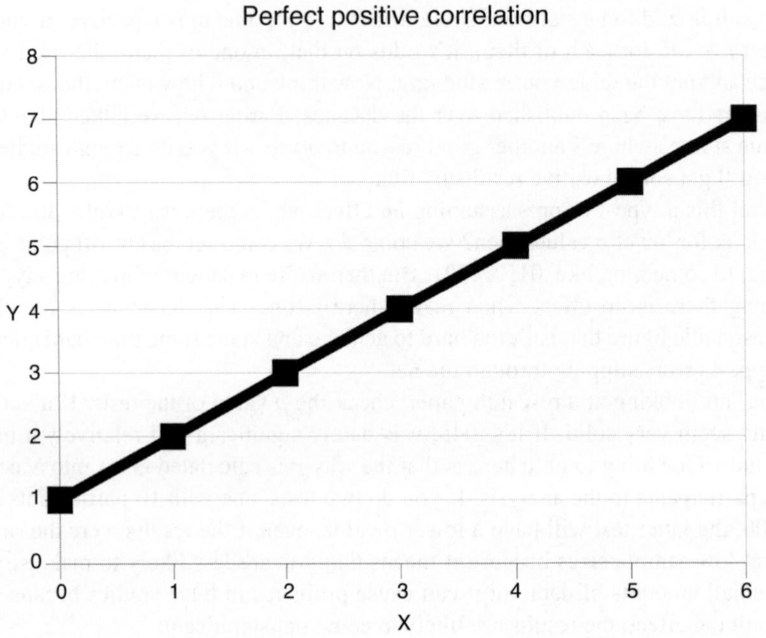

Perfect positive correlation

Figure 3.1 In a perfect positive correlation, the data points all fall on a straight line

You might be able to think of counter examples to the ones above: the weirdo who wears seven layers of clothing in the summer; the tall, skinny guy who doesn't weigh much. If these variables correlate, why do these counter examples exist? It comes down to the strength of the correlation. Stronger correlations have fewer counter examples. A perfect correlation means that a high score in one variable always means there will be a high score in the other one and a low score in one always means a low score in another (assuming it's a perfect *positive* correlation of course).

The 'correlation coefficient', known as r, tells you how close the correlation is to being perfect and whether the correlation is positive or negative. You will come across r very often from now on, so you'd better get to know it. In journal papers, r is reported as a number between -1 and 1. It is never outside this range. When r is 1, this means that there is a perfect *positive* correlation between the two variables. If you were to plot the scores of the variables on a scatter graph, they would all fall directly on a straight line, as shown in Figure 3.1.

When r is -1, this means that there is a perfect *negative* correlation between the two variables. Again, the points would fall on a straight line on a scatter graph, only a negative correlation would look like the one in Figure 3.2.

When r is 0, this means there is no correlation. A scatter graph might look something like Figure 3.3.

As you can see, there is no obvious place you could put a line in this graph. You could put it in any number of places and there would be no reason to choose one over any other. Hence,

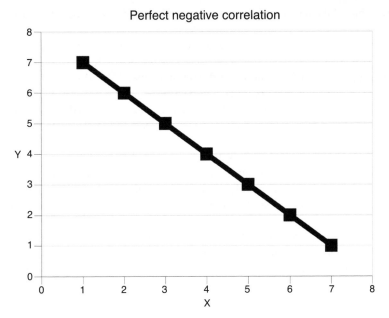

Figure 3.2 In a perfect negative correlation, the data points also fall on a straight line but along the opposite diagonal

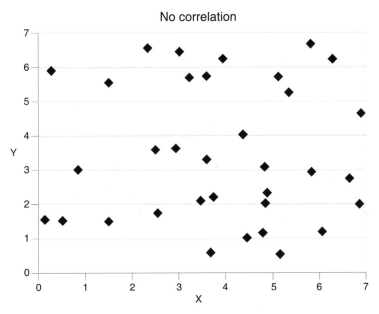

Figure 3.3 There is no correlation between these two variables

there is no relationship. If the data points were on a vertical or horizontal line, this is also no correlation.

In psychology, you will probably never come across a perfect correlation. This is because psychological variables cannot be measured with perfect accuracy. If I fill out a questionnaire measuring my extraversion, it will be slightly different today than if I had done it yesterday, even though I'm the same person and not much will be different about my personality today. Maybe my mood would be slightly better, maybe I'd be tired, maybe I'd read the wording of one of the questions differently – little things like this would get in the way of perfect measurement.

Because of this, psychologists do not look for perfect correlations. In fact, if they find any correlation at all they are usually quite happy, although ahead are some 'rules of thumb' as to whether a correlation is considered strong or weak. These are just guidelines, however, and not set in stone. The value of different strength correlations will be determined by theory.

Figure 3.4 shows a weak correlation where $r = .3$. As you can see, the data points are very widely spread but a slight pattern is starting to develop. There are fewer scores in the upper-left and lower-right areas, which gives a weak but noticeable upward trend to the data.

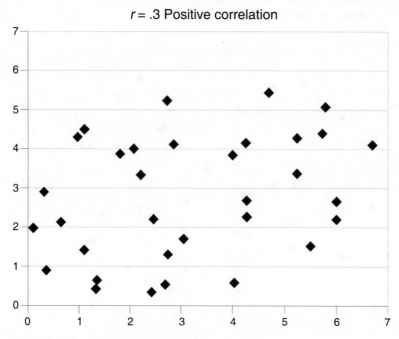

Figure 3.4 A weak positive correlation

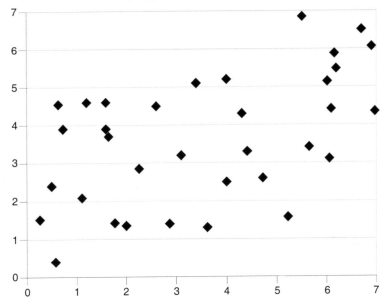

Figure 3.5 A moderate positive correlation

Figure 3.5 shows a moderate correlation, where $r = .5$. The pattern is much clearer here, as most of the data points fall on a channel going from the bottom left to the top right. But the channel is quite wide, so there's a lot of variation and a few scores fall a little outside of the main pack pattern. Still, this would be seen as a decent research result.

Figure 3.6 shows a strong correlation, where $r = .7$. Now the pattern is obvious, although the scores fall on a slightly wide channel, so there's still some variation there.

Figure 3.7 shows a very strong correlation of .9. The pattern is clear; all the points lie on the same thin channel, with no scores outside of the pattern. If two variables correlate this highly, they are quite possibly the same thing, but measured in two different ways. Correlations this high are rare indeed in psychology.

How correlations are reported in journals

In a journal paper, you might see something like this:

$$r = .36, p < .001$$

A p value should always accompany the value of r. In this case, the variables are correlated, if fairly weakly, and, since the p value is very low, it is unlikely that this correlation is down to chance.

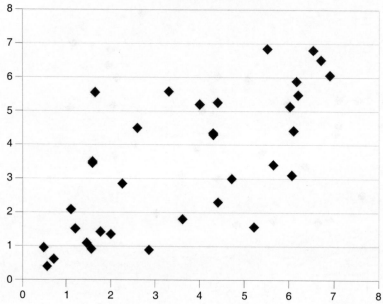

Figure 3.6 A strong positive correlation

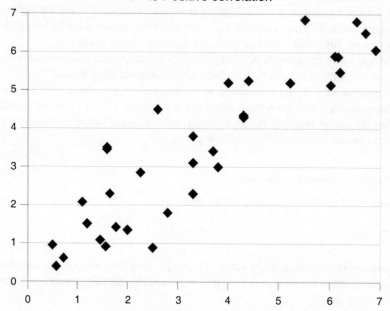

Figure 3.7 A very strong correlation; in fact, the variables may even be the same thing

Remember, scientists generally do experiments to find cause and effect relationships between variables. Here is an important point that you must understand:

Correlation does not imply causality.

The fact that two variables correlate does not mean that one variable has a causal influence on the other. It might be true; it might not: you just cannot tell without manipulating a variable and seeing what happens. For example, recall the negative relationship between temperature and amount of clothes. With a correlation, all we know is that these variables are related. You and I both know that temperature is the variable that is exerting the causal effect. It's absurd to think that removing clothes has a causal effect on environmental temperature. But it's only absurd because we already know this.

What about another example: the positive correlation between income and happiness? Now things are not quite so obvious. Maybe money does make people happier. You could see that being true; you can buy new things, put food on the plate, and so on. But on the other hand, you can imagine that upbeat, happy, people might earn more money. Maybe likeable people are more likely to get jobs and promotions, make more sales or bounce back from setbacks than grouches. Because correlations only look at data from one point in time (so-called cross-sectional evidence), you don't know what causes what. You'll remember from our discussion of the scientific method starting on page 7, that it's only the design of the experiment that allows us to find cause–effect relationships – never the type of analysis.

When you get a correlation, there are a few possibilities for cause–effect relationships:

1. Variable A causes variable B (e.g., money causes happiness).
2. Variable B causes variable A (e.g., happiness causes money).
3. Variable C causes variable A and B (e.g., self-confidence causes money and happiness).

Possibility 3 is often called the third variable problem and it comes up quite a lot in psychology. When you see a study that only uses a correlation analysis, know that the study cannot determine which of these three options is correct. You need other evidence, either experimental studies to know for sure or a lot of converging evidence from different research designs if you can't do experiments for some reason.

A great example of such a case is the cannabis and schizophrenia link. Does cannabis cause schizophrenia or not? Hotly debated by academics and often misinterpreted by the press, this is a contentious issue. The whole thing could be solved by a good-quality experimental study. I would get 200 people who have never used any kind of drug before, tell 100 of them to smoke cannabis everyday for five years and the other one to go about their business as usual. There would be no point giving them some kind of placebo cannabis, as they'd soon figure out it was a placebo when it had no effect. At the end of the test I'd see if more people in the cannabis group had developed schizophrenia.

Unfortunately, psychologists aren't allowed to do studies like this. It kind of spoils all the fun but it's for a good reason! How can one ethically justify doing a study where you are hypothesizing that a good number of your participants will develop a debilitating mental illness for the rest of their lives, because of what you did to them? You can't, and ethics committees won't permit you to do the study (although I'll leave it to you to decide whether that's through moral sense or fear of litigation).

So you need converging evidence in cases like this. Take data from people aged 5, and check on them 20 years later. Split them into groups; those that took up cannabis and those that didn't, and see which group reports the most psychosis. This is longitudinal evidence and it gives you a stronger idea of what the cause and effect *might* be, although it still does not give you cause and effect. Because you are not manipulating the variables, you don't know whether people developed schizophrenia first and then turned to cannabis as a way of dealing with the symptoms. Or whether the Jolly Green Giant is secretly running around giving people schizophrenia *and* cannabis. One just doesn't know (and before you write in, yes, of course I am aware that the last example was completely ridiculous; I'm just making a point. I don't *really* think the Jolly Green Giant would have anything to do with drugs).

Main point to remember – the only way to determine cause and effect is to use an experimental design. A correlation between two variables can tell you that they are related in some way but it does not imply causality.

Regression

A regression is very similar in principle to a correlation and, since they can both be displayed with a scatter diagram, you might assume that they were the same thing if you didn't know the difference. The difference is that, with a regression, we are trying to predict the score of one variable (called the target, criterion or dependent variable) with what we know about another one (called the predictor or independent variable). It also allows us to calculate the predicted change in the DV as a result of a one-unit increase or decrease in the IV. If needed, we can use more than one criterion variable, in which case we'd call it a multiple regression.

With a regression, we are in a sense assuming there is some influence going on between the variables but, like correlation, a regression cannot tell us anything about what is influencing what.

Imagine you and I are organizational psychologists and we want to find out how best to predict the productivity of our client's employees. There's a correlation between job satisfaction and productivity – that is, people who are satisfied with their jobs tend to perform better than those who aren't. So we might start there. But this isn't a perfect correlation – it's possible to not like your job and still be good at it or to really like it but slack off a lot. So if we tried to predict productivity based on what we know about job satisfaction, we'd probably guess incorrectly quite often, because although the two variables correlate, the variance in job satisfaction – that is, how much difference there is in job satisfaction between people in a given group – is not similar enough to the variance in productivity to account for all of it. If we take out the variance that the two variables share, there is still a lot left over.

Productivity/job satisfaction – variance shared

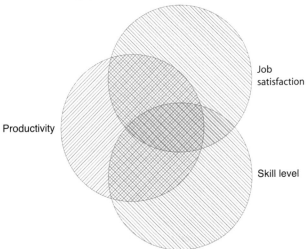

Figure 3.8 The variance that productivity and job satisfaction might share

A regression can tell us how much of the variation in one variable can be accounted for by variation in another, and this is given as a percentage of the overall variance. A diagram might help: see Figure 3.8.

Here, we might be able to account for, say, 36 per cent (made-up figure) of the variance in productivity using information that we have on job satisfaction. If we want to predict more variance, we need to add more variables to the regression. It would then become a *multiple regression*, which is quite common in psychology. Maybe we could add in some measure of skill level (see Figure 3.9).

Productivity/job satisfaction/skill level – variance shared

Figure 3.9 The variance that productivity shares with job satisfaction and skill level

Now we can account for much more variance and therefore make a more accurate prediction of someone's productivity. But there's still a lot of variance left over, so we might want to do more research, adding more variables to our model. Over a number of studies we could test many different variables and, if we eventually create a model that accounts for a large amount of variance, we'd have a very good chance of knowing how productive someone was if we knew about these other variables. We'd also know how 'important' these are to productivity; that is, which account for the most variance.

If we then did some experimental studies to determine causal links between our predictor and criterion variables, we'd have a good model to work from when advising people, designing interventions, and so on. We'd be able to increase our consulting fees too!

Of course, during our research we'd come across variables that didn't add much to our model. A very common use of multiple regression is to see if a new variable can tell us anything new, on top of what we already know. Say we wants to see if motivation can account for any further variance. If we did this, we might discover that motivation does not account for any further variance; perhaps because the impact of motivation is included within things we've already measured. Although motivation may correlate with productivity, it might not account for much more variance than our model does already. Again, this is a made-up example to make the point and, technically, this diagram would have to be in three dimensions but see Figure 3.10 to see how this might look. Notice how the motivation circle, in the middle, is mostly already accounted for by the other two circles, except for that little bit that the arrow points to – that's the only unique contribution it makes in this made up example.

There are a few different types of multiple regression, which differ in the ways that each variable is entered into the regression equation and how the variance accounted for is assigned to each predictor variable. This is a more advanced consideration that I'm not going to go into here but it might be useful to look into the differences between these different types (standard, hierarchical, statistical) at some point in your studies. If you take an advanced stats or research methods class (which you should if you can), you'll cover it there.

So that's an introduction to regression – the aim is to be able to predict the value of one variable using the score of another variable. With a multiple regression, you can use more predictors, which allows you to:

- account for more variance
- see which IVs are important and . . .
- see which aren't (relative to each other)
- see how the prediction of a variable can be improved (or not) by adding different predictor variables
- learn how the predictors relate to each another.

Eventually, we hope, you will build a model that accounts for a large amount of variance in the thing you're studying, so that you understand that particular thing better; maybe just for theoretical reasons but maybe to help you design treatments or interventions around your model.

Productivity/job satisfaction/skill level/motivation – variance shared

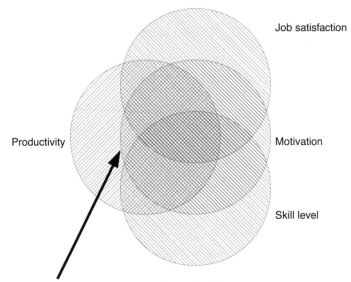

Unique variance accounted for by motivation

Figure 3.10 Although motivation does correlate with productivity, it also correlates with job satisfaction and skill level so, in this made-up example, our model already accounts for motivation indirectly

How to read regression statistics in journal papers

Unlike the bivariate correlation, where you just get r and p, with regression you get a few more statistics. You still get a p value, which tells you the same thing – the probability that the results you got were down to chance, assuming the null hypothesis to be true, but you also get the following:

- r^2
- adjusted r^2
- multiple r^2
- b
- *beta* (β)
- c

r^2

r^2 tells you how much variance in the DV is explained by the IV. It is, as you might have guessed, the square of the correlation coefficient between the two variables. It's given as a percentage of the overall amount of variance in the whole of your data.

Adjusted r^2

Adjusted r^2 is simply a slightly more conservative estimate of what r^2 might be, which takes into account things like sample size. This is the figure you should look out for in papers and the one that is normally reported.

Multiple r^2

This is multiple regression version of r^2, which tells you how much variance in the DV is predicted by all the IVs together. Sometimes it is reported simply as R^2, without the 'multiple' prefix.

b

b is the *regression coefficient*. It tells you how strongly your IV influences the DV. Specifically, it tells you how much change in the target variable your model predicts, following a one-unit change in the IV. The value of *b* also corresponds to the slope of the regression line in a graph, in a similar way that *r* corresponds roughly to a line of best fit that you might draw in a correlation. If you're doing a multiple regression, you get a *b* for each IV and it represents that change in DV score when that IV score is changed by 1 unit while all the other IV scores are held constant.

   b is *unstandardized*, which means that you can't compare the *b* in one paper to the *b* in another paper (although the associated *p* values can be compared across papers/tests). To compare *b*, you will need . . .

beta (b)

Beta, or (β) is *b* that has been standardized for comparison across studies. It is measured in standard deviations: an increase in the IV of one standard deviation equates to an increase of β standard deviations in the DV. Again, if it's a multiple regression, this assumes that all the other IVs are held constant.

c

You will rarely come across *c* in journals, as it is not usually necessary to report it, but it is used in the regression equation so it's worth mentioning. It is simply the value of the DV when the IV is zero. Typically, this is where the regression line crosses the *y* axis of the graph. It's often called the constant or the intercept.

   Regression analyses are reported in various ways. Because a paper will often report many tests, the results may be presented as a chart. In this case, you'll probably get a column for β, one for r^2 and one for the *p* value. Or you might see them written out, like this:

The multiple *r* with 4 and 12,267 *df* was .61 ($p < .0001$) and the standardized β were: job satisfaction, .32; skill level, .24; salary .21; and motivation, .15.

Let's break this down. Here we have a multiple regression. Multiple *r* was .61 – so that's the correlation between all IVs together and the DV. If we square this, we get multiple r^2, which tells us the percentage of variance in the DV that the model can account for – in this case, 37 per cent – a decent amount. We have two figures for degrees of freedom (*df*), which are 4 and 12,267. A detailed discussion of degrees of freedom is outside the scope of this book but, from them, you can learn the number of IVs in the study (the first figure) and the approximate number of participants (the second figure).

From this wording we can find out a lot. The researchers want to predict productivity based on job satisfaction, skill level, motivation and salary. This was a huge study with over 12,000 participants. The model overall accounts for 37 per cent of the variance in productivity, with job satisfaction being the most strongly related to it; at least, when the other three variables are held constant. If job satisfaction increases by one standard deviation, productivity is predicted to increases by .32 standard deviations. They are highly unlikely to have achieved this result by chance as the *p* value is very low (although the massive sample size probably played a large part in that).

t test

The *t* test is the third of the four common statistical tests we're looking at. A *t* test is a way of finding out whether there is a difference between the means of two sets of data. This could involve comparing a treatment group with a placebo control group, testing the same group of people at two different time points, testing males against females, and so on.

You might think: why don't you just work out the total or the average for each group and see which one is highest? You can't do just this, because, in psychology, there is extra special emphasis on whether the difference is statistically significant.

If two groups in an analysis have different means, there are two possibilities:

- the hypothesis is correct
- the hypothesis is not correct.

In other words, just because the two groups have different averages, this does not mean that the hypothesis is correct. The results might just be a fluke and it would be useful to know what is the probability of this. This is what a *t* test tells you.

Here's an example. David Strohmetz and his colleagues (Strohmetz, Rind, Fisher and Lynn, 2002) wanted to know whether waitresses could get better tips by giving customers a piece of chocolate along with the cheque. So they used an experimental design with two conditions – in one, the waitress just gave customers a bill and, in the other, she gave a bill and a piece of chocolate. So that's a pretty standard experimental design with random assignment to either an experimental condition or a control condition.

They did this for four days and totalled up the amount of tips that customers gave. In the end, the waitresses did get more tips when they gave the piece of chocolate – they were tipped 18 per cent of the bill on average, while the customers who didn't get the chocolate tipped 15 per cent of the bill on average.

But this mean difference does not necessarily provide support for the hypothesis. Perhaps, just by pure chance, more people in the chocolate condition happened to be generous people and would have tipped more regardless of whether they got a chocolate. Or maybe, by chance, the people who didn't get the chocolate were all in bad moods that day. There is always the possibility that the results of a study were a complete fluke finding. Let's see what the full results were:

This hypothesis was supported, $t(90) = 5.25$, $p < .0001$, effect size $r = .048$.

(Strohmetz et al. 2002)

The figure in brackets is the degrees of freedom. Again, explaining that is beyond the scope of this little book and trying to find out will only make your head hurt. I've read advanced statistics books that only gloss over the topic, so don't worry. All you need to know for practical purposes is that it is the approximate number of participants in the study, in total. I doubt this will come up in a test but check with your teachers to make sure. If so, find out more, but I imagine this is pretty much all you'll need to know.

The next figure, 5.25, is the value of t itself. The bigger the t the bigger the difference between groups. The t statistic can also be a minus figure (e.g., $t = -5.25$) but this simply means that the variables have been put into the equation the opposite way around.

After that, we have a p value. We discussed this earlier but, just because it bears repeating, the p value gives you the probability that the results were obtained by chance, assuming the null hypothesis to be correct, and we're looking for a figure lower than .05. In this case, the probability that Strohmetz and his team got these results by chance is less than 0.001 per cent – a solid finding. If their p value was closer to the .05 level, maybe .047, we would interpret the results with a little more caution. Often, a higher p value stems from having a low number of participants and the study may need to be replicated using a larger sample size. Usually, you would want to see at least 30 participants in each group, preferably 40, ideally 50+.

We also have another statistic: r, which you'll remember is the same statistic used in correlations. However, in this case, r is not referring to a correlation but an effect size. We'll cover effect sizes in more detail soon.

ANOVA

ANOVA is short for ANalysis Of VAriance. Sometimes you want to compare the means of more than two groups. Sometimes a study has three groups; sometimes many more. You can't do a t test in these cases, so you'd use an ANOVA.

In principle, ANOVA does the same thing as the *t* test – it tells you whether there is a significant difference between the means of the groups in the analysis. Actually, if you used an ANOVA on only two groups, you'd get equivalent results as a *t* test and the same *p* value.

So when you see an ANOVA in a journal, it's because the researchers are hypothesizing that there's a difference between three or more groups. These groups are called the *levels* of an IV – for example, a study might test the effect of a drug at 10mg, 20mg, 30mg and 0mg (control group) to see if there is a tailing off of the drug's effects beyond a certain dosage. That would be four levels of the IV.

The statistic for the ANOVA is F, also called the F-ratio, and as always you get a *p* value which means the same thing as with any test – the probability that the result (or greater) came about by chance, assuming the null hypothesis to be true.

ANOVA works because it is possible to split the variance into two partitions – between-groups variance and within-groups variance. If the means of the groups are different, the between-groups variance will be a very different figure to the within-groups variance. F is the ratio between the between-groups variance and the within-groups variance and, therefore, the bigger the difference in means, the bigger the F will be. The actual logic of how the F ratio is calculated is a little technical and I recommend that you spend a little time every day going over your statistics textbooks until you are comfortable with it.

The weakness of an ANOVA is that it can only tell us that there is a difference in the means *somewhere*; not which means are significantly different from which others. To find this out, it is necessary to do follow-up comparisons, which might mean separate *t* tests on each combination of group or a specialized test like a Tukey test.

Multi-factor ANOVA

ANOVA has some useful advantages over *t* tests, such as being able to analyze more than one IV and tell us how they interact with each other and how any interactions affect the DV.

If you recall, we can do a similar thing with a regression and when we use more than one IV it's called a multiple regression. It's not surprising that we can do the same with ANOVA, since statistically they are the same test. ANOVA also gets a slightly modified name in this case, depending on how many IVs there are. When we use two independent variables in an ANOVA, it's called a two-factor ANOVA. With three IVs, it's a three-factor ANOVA, and so on. Variable and factor mean the same thing here.

Each one of the factors in a multi-factor ANOVA can have as many levels as is required. This can get very complicated but I'll just use a two-factor ANOVA in the example below, because once you get this, it's not a great stretch of logic to understand all multi-factor ANOVAs.

Say we're testing the effects of two kinds of music – heavy metal and jazz - on happiness, and we want to see if there's a gender difference. The two IVs, or factors of our ANOVA, are gender and music type. Our DV is happiness. Our two factors each have two levels, or groups – gender has male and female; music type has heavy metal and jazz. We'd call this a 2 × 2 ANOVA – two factors, two levels each. If you wanted, you could also call it a 'two-way

ANOVA' or a 'two-by-two ANOVA'. If we had three types of music, it would be a 3 × 2 ANOVA – two factors: one with two levels, one with three.

A little advance warning: multi-factor ANOVAs can get a little extreme sometimes. You might occasionally see something like a 4 × 7 × 8 × 8 ANOVA. This is more complex but the format is exactly the same – each separate number represents a factor, a different variable being studied. So there we have four factors. Whatever each number is, represents the number of levels that factor has. Here, one factor has four levels, the next seven, the last two have eight levels.

Main effects and interactions

With a multi-factor ANOVA, it is possible to investigate *main effects*, which are the effects of each variable individually, and *interactions*, in which the effect of an IV is different at different levels of another factor. It sounds complicated but this example will help.

Imagine the figures in Table 3.1 are the happiness scores in our experiment on music and gender. In this example, females love heavy metal, while males prefer jazz.

First lets talk about main effects. A main effect is what you get when you take the average scores of one IV and look at it individually. In this example, the main effects of gender and music type on happiness happen to be the same – 4.5. See Tables 3.2 and Table 3.3.

We could have done this study with only one IV. Let's say we didn't use gender as an IV. Since we'd only have the results in Table 3.2 to look at, we wouldn't see how happy heavy metal makes females or how happy jazz makes males. We'd conclude that heavy metal and jazz make people equally happy.

Table 3.1 The results of our fictional music and happiness study

	Heavy metal	Jazz
Males	3	6
Females	6	3

Table 3.2 The main effect of music on happiness

Males	4.5
Females	4.5

Table 3.3 The main effect of gender on happiness

Heavy metal	4.5
Jazz	4.5

Music, gender and happiness interaction

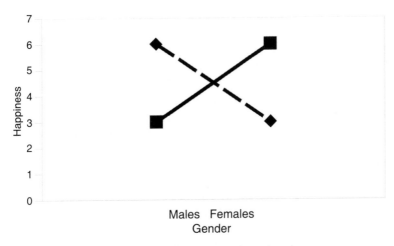

Figure 3.11 Graph of the interaction in our music study

This is where interactions come in. They tell us whether the effect of an IV on the DV is different depending on what level of another IV you're looking at. In other words, they tell us whether the effect of heavy metal and jazz on happiness depends on whether you're talking about males or females.

There's a very simple way of finding out if there's an interaction in a multi-factor ANOVA and that is to use a plot. Take a look at Figure 3.11. The DV (happiness) is on the *y* axis, the levels of one IV (gender) are on the *x* axis: each line represents the levels of the second IV (music type).

Any time you make a graph like Figure 3.11 and the lines are not parallel, that indicates an interaction. In this case, music and gender are interacting to have their effect on happiness. However, like all tests in psychology, you have to check for statistical significance. In a multi-factor ANOVA, you get an F value for each main effect and for the interaction, and everything gets a *p* value.

In some areas of psychology, multi-factor ANOVAs are more common than in others. Cognitive psychology is particularly fond of them but, overall, you are most likely to encounter the one-way ANOVA described earlier.

The main point to remember is that when you see an ANOVA, researchers want to know whether there is a statistically significant difference in the means of several groups. If it's a multi-factor ANOVA, they are testing more than one IV at the same time and they also want to know whether the interaction between these IVs has an effect on the DV.

Effect size

For numerous reasons, many statisticians lament the focus on statistical significance in psychology. They have a point. The cult-like focus on statistical significance is not justified by its usefulness. It is only one part of the story told by the data.

Remember this: just because something is statistically significant, that doesn't make it *psychologically significant*. Null-hypothesis significance testing is flawed in many ways which are too technical to go into here but your stats textbooks will have more information. We discussed one example earlier – the tendency for large sample sizes to produce statistically significant results even though the differences between the means might be tiny. Indeed, if you dig around in a large but completely randomly generated data set for long enough, you might well find some statistically significant results.

Because of this, we need to look at the data from other angles, such as by checking something called the *effect size*. The effect size is a measure of the size of an effect (surprisingly enough) but it is also standardized, just like the beta value we discussed earlier. This means that effect sizes from different studies using different scales and measures can be compared.

The most popular effect size statistics are Cohen's d and Pearson's r. The latter, you'll remember, is usually used as a measure of correlation – the strength of the relationship between two variables. It is used in a similar way here, in that a higher r signifies a stronger effect (larger difference between means or more variance accounted for). It might be confusing to see an experimental analysis using a statistic primarily found in correlation studies but just be aware that it can be used in both.

Effect sizes are of vital importance in psychology, because they help you separate something that is only statistically significant from something that is psychologically significant. Although statistically significant results might sound impressive and help to get papers published in journals, if the phenomenon under inspection isn't having much influence in the real world, the effect is not necessarily worth getting excited about (although try telling that to newspaper headline writers).

So look out for the effect sizes in journal papers, and use the following figures as *guidelines* (see Table 3.4).

As before, you can square r to get the amount of variance accounted for – so an effect size of $r = .5$ accounts for 25 per cent of the variance. Another thing to keep in mind is that values

Table 3.4 Effect size guidelines

Statistic	Small	Medium	Large
d	0.2	0.5	0.8
r	.1	.24	.37

of r do not fall on a linear scale – in other words, $r = .6$ is not twice as big as $r = .3$. To compare r in this way you need to square it. However, Cohen's d is on a linear scale, so you can compare d directly. Generally, r tends to be used when researchers are concerned about the amount of variance explained and d is usually used when mean differences are the concern. However, either can technically be used and it is possible to convert one into the other.

4   Get the information in

We're moving from the foundations of the discipline of psychology into the study skills that will help you succeed in it and this first section is pretty self-explanatory. There's a lot of information in books, articles and other peoples' heads that you need to get into your head. So, the better you are at finding and assimilating the information you need and the better you get at ignoring information that you don't need, the more successful your studies will be. This chapter is broken into the following:

- research skills
- reading skills
- note-taking skills
- listening to lectures and papers.

Research skills

When you have a new topic to research, I recommend that you don't dive straight into journal papers. As an overall rule, start with the broader, more general sources of information and then move towards the specific. For example, don't read about how cognitive theories overlap with other areas until you understand the theories independently and don't read about specific experiments if there is a meta-analysis you can read first. Getting a good bird's eye view will help you to see how all the specifics relate to each other. However, if you feel you have gained a strong enough overview from the lecture or prior knowledge, you can skip this step.

Move through the following steps in this order.

Video

The first thing to do is to get a list of the major players in the field. Look at your recommended reading list and note the names of the researchers that crop up often and the ones who wrote the seminal papers. Then go to the following websites and search for their names:

- ted.com
- bigthink.com

- youtube.com
- video.google.com

You can also do a 'normal' Google search, with 'their name in quotes' + 'the topic area' + 'video'. For example:

'Carol Dweck' + 'mindset' + 'video'

Putting quotes around single words will cause Google to ignore synonyms of that word – if nothing useful comes up, try the same search without the quote marks. By doing this, you'll very often get a 20–60 minute overview of the exact topic you're researching, with descriptions of the evidence and maybe their thoughts and opinions on the subject too, which can help.

You can also do the same but without a researchers name:

'working memory' 'video'

This can bring up some useful stuff but be sure to check the credentials of the speaker!

Researcher blogs

Search for the names of the major players in Google to see if they have a personal blog. Many researchers maintain personal blogs at: psychologytoday.com. If that doesn't bring up anything useful, they may have a personal website or a profile on their university website that contains links to articles they have written for the lay audience. Look these up too.

If you find a blog, skim through their archive and see if they have anything to say about the topic you're researching. Take particular note of any general thoughts, criticisms, arguments and opinions, as these might be relevant but just haven't made it into a journal article yet.

Popular books

Do any of the major players have a popular book on the subject that you can get from your library? If so, get it, but read the section on reading (page 55) before you get started on it. Very often, popular books will be filled with stories and anecdotes that are entertaining but not relevant to your studies – you'll need to learn to cherry pick the information you need from a book.

Research papers: recommended reading

Once you have a decent overview of the topic, you'll need to move to the journal papers. The first papers you should read are the ones on the recommended reading list for this subject.

More often than not, these papers will play a role in any assignments and exams you have, so start here. Be aware that some lecturers are more enthusiastic about recommending papers than others. If the reading list is particularly large, it's unlikely you'll need to read every single one, so ask the lecturer which are the most important ones to focus on.

Research papers: further reading

Once you have read the recommended papers, where do you go next? Reading the recommended papers and their reference lists should give you some ideas, as will searching the PsycINFO® or PsycARTICLES® databases. There are some further ideas on finding journal papers below but the main thing is to find a balance between following your own thoughts and inquiries and sticking to the subject matter so you are prepared for the exams and essays. If the authors of a paper reference another paper that sounds interesting or useful, highlight it and check it later.

Discussion lists

Most academic disciplines have email lists or discussion boards through which the researchers keep in contact, discuss ideas and talk about very recent (even unpublished) research. If you Google 'sub-field' 'discussion list' or 'email discussion list' you should find them. These can be an absolute gold mine for up-to-date information on a field.

How to find elusive papers

At some point you'll desperately need a particular journal. When Google Scholar fails, you may search for the title of the paper and discover that it is almost impossible to obtain. You even might be tempted to pay the US$15+ that most journals charge for a single paper. Don't! In 99.9 per cent of the cases, it's out there; you just need to know where to look.

Step 1: Online databases

Start by searching the online databases that you can access through your university. If you have an ATHENS account or similar, PsycINFO and PsycARTICLES are the big databases worth looking at. Also, register at sciencedirect.com and check there. These, along with your university's intranet portal, should be your first ports of call.

Step 2: Google Scholar

Search at scholar.google.com – search for the full title of the paper first and, if that doesn't work, just search for a snip of it that has no question marks or colons in it. Sometimes a paper will be there but searching for the full title doesn't bring it up for some reason. If it comes up in the results but there's no PDF file, click the 'all x versions' link at the bottom of the entry.

This will bring up a list of all the locations that Google knows for the paper – one of which might have the full document available for download.

Step 3: 'Normal' Google

When Google Scholar fails, search for the title of the paper in normal Google. Sometimes this will bring up a page hosting the paper or the author's personal website where you can download it.

Step 4: Authors' websites

Some researchers maintain websites where you can download every paper they've ever written, for free. Or some times they are hosted on their university pages. Google the names of each of the researchers in the paper and check all their personal websites and faculty homepages, just in case the Google search didn't pick them up already (which happens).

Step 5: Email the authors

If none of the authors has the paper available for download (sometimes, annoyingly, they just have a list of papers without download links), email the first author and ask if they have a PDF they could send you. Say you really need the paper for your research. Don't write a seven-page explanation of why you want it and don't be surprised if you get a reply with no content, just the paper as an attachment. They are not being rude, they just get about a million emails a day. The times I've had to do this, I've always received a reply. If the first author can't or won't send you a copy, email the second author, and so on.

Step 6: Ask your peers

Email/ask your fellow students who are doing the same assignment if they have it. Also ask the lecturer who gave the class if they have it (mention that you have tried the above steps so that they can see the effort you're putting in and won't think you are being lazy!).

Step 7: Hard copies

Check your university's holdings to see if they have a paper version of it. This is unlikely if it hasn't shown up in the online searches but possible. By the way, the reason this is step 6 and not step 1 is that this is the first point you'll have to actually leave your desk!

Step 8: Other universities

Check with other universities. Search their online catalogues first, to see if they have the journal you want. Obviously, start with the closest one to you and move outwards. I don't know about the USA but here in the UK there are schemes to allow you to access other libraries and to get books out (sconul.ac.uk/) and, failing that, most will allow you to join as a guest for the day (sometimes for a price).

Reading skills

So far, so good. You've got an overview of the topic and you've located some important literature to read. Let me guess what your next steps would be:

1.   Take the book or paper and open to it to the first page.
2.   Start on the first word of the first page, then read the word next to it.
3.   Continue to the end of the book or paper.

When I've spoken to people about how they read, probably over 95 per cent say they read like this. And why wouldn't you? It seems perfectly normal and logical; the only problem is, it's probably the most inefficient way to study!

It's perfect if you're reading a novel, because the writer has carefully crafted an experience for you with their words and the idea is for you to go on the journey exactly as they have presented it. But studying is not the same as reading for pleasure. Your aim is not to experience the writer's highly refined literary prowess; it's to extract the information you need while ignoring that which you don't need. Most of the writing in the books and papers you read is irrelevant to you – for example, introductions to papers in the same area are often very similar and you might only need one or two chapters from a book. Just because the book is on the same broad topic as your essay does not mean that you need to read it all.

Here, we can take some tips from speed reading. I don't really like the term 'speed reading', because it conjures images of people flicking through books at lightning speed, taking it all in. For our purposes, this is pretty much fantasy, because as you read you'll have to stop and reflect, think about what the author means or relate it to something else you've read. Reading isn't a passive process of sucking the words from a book into your brain. Maybe 'effective reading' is a better term, because while it can be helpful to increase the actual speed at which you read, the main benefit is in knowing what parts not to read and engaging with the parts you do read.

Effective reading

The general principle is the same as with studying in general. Get a broad overview, then move to the specifics. So you'll read results, discussions, conclusions, etc., first. This gives you the context into which to fit the rest of the information. Think of this as creating a load of hooks on to which you can put the rest of the information – it's much easier to read this way than to get the information first, then the hooks.

Step 1: Preparation

Before you even pick the book up, think about what you want from it. Are you reading it for a particular class or assignment? What questions do you want answered? What are you unsure about and need clarification on? As I said before, don't just pick up the book and start reading but take a few minutes to define what you want and what you are looking for. Write your questions in the corner of your page – never start reading without knowing what you want to get out of it. Also, note the time you'll read for; as we'll discuss later, you should not study for more than 40–50 minutes without taking a break.

Step 2: Overview

Pick up the book and browse through it, just as you would if you picked it off the shelf in a bookshop. Just have a quick flick through so you know what you're dealing with. Then look at the contents to see which parts interest you. Are there any chapters you can definitely rule out as being irrelevant? Circle the chapter numbers of the ones you definitely need to read and strike through the ones that you don't need. If there are any chapters that are not relevant to your identified purpose for reading the book but you just want to read out of interest, don't read them! At least, not right now. Make a note somewhere and come back to the book in your leisure time.

Step 3: Skimming

At this point, you may have already identified parts you won't be reading. The next step is to skim through the chapters you think are relevant – or might be. Your goal is still not to read! You are simply selecting and rejecting the parts you will read in detail later. There are several ways to do this:

- Use the speed reading techniques described later.
- Read only the first sentence and last sentence of each paragraph.
- Use a tracker (see page 58) and move much faster than you can actually read. You'll only pick up the odd word but you will get the rough gist and know if you need that section.

As you skim through, mark the sections you'll want to read later. Don't underline – that will only slow you down. Just put a vertical line in the margin next to the section you want. If you need the whole page, put a slash or x or something in the top corner of the page. If it's not your book, use a pencil, mark lightly and erase your handiwork afterwards.

As you're skimming, look out for filler material. Very often with books (particularly when written for the lay audience), you'll get one paragraph that explains a certain idea or study, then a few more that explain it in a different way or use an anecdote to explain it. These have been put into the book to help people understand the idea better. If you already understand the idea, these paragraphs are useless to you – skip them.

As you do this, you will sometimes come across an interesting section of the book and you'll find yourself dipping in to read normally. This will happen, so don't worry when it does. As soon as you recognize what you're doing, just mark the section and go back to skimming.

Many times after the skimming process I have found my questions answered, without need for further reading. Or sometimes I realize the book is not actually suitable for what I want. I wonder how many hours of my life I've freed up by not reading books in the traditional manner.

Step 4: Reading

At step 4, we can now begin reading! Go back to page 1 and start flicking through the book. As soon as you get to a section you have marked, read it. Then flick through to the next part. The next section on speed-reading will be of further use here, as will the section on critical thinking on page 78. It's at this point you can start taking notes as you read. Try to avoid taking notes while skimming, unless you can identify a big theme or important idea. More on note taking on page 59.

As I've already mentioned, reading isn't simply the sucking of information from a book to your brain. You have to think about how it relates to other areas in psychology; how is it similar, how different; do any other theories challenge it and can it be synthesized with other theories? Also, challenge the material – is the evidence sufficient, can you think of alternative ideas or interpretations? Don't think that just because it's a published piece of work that it has to be correct. Challenge and question everything you read – even the book you are reading now!

Speed reading

Although eliminating the excess is the best way to speed up your reading, there are times, of course, when you're not skimming and not sat reflecting but just reading. This is when it is useful to be able to actually read the words faster; and you'd be surprised at how easy it is to increase your speed. But you won't have to take my word for it; I'll prove it to you. This section contains instructions and exercises to increase your reading speed without negatively affecting comprehension. It won't take you to superhuman levels but it will help you to sharpen the saw.

First, you need to get a baseline measure of your speed. Get a non-technical book to practise on; count the total number of words on five random lines and divide that number by five. That's your average words per line. Now set a timer and read as you normally would for two minutes, noting the points at which you start and stop reading. Add up the number of lines in between, multiply that figure by your average words per line and you have your baseline reading speed.

Next, spend an hour or so practising the following techniques:

- don't read the whole line
- use a tracker
- overclock
- practise!

Don't read the whole line

When you read, your eyes don't move across the text in a smooth line. They make little jumps, called 'saccades' between several fixation points. Your peripheral vision picks up a little text to the left (maybe one word) of the fixation point and a little more to the right (maybe three words). Reverse these figures if your native language moves from right to left.

We can save a little time by starting each line one or two words in from the left margin and finishing three or four words from the right. Our peripheral vision will pick up the rest – if we read the whole line, we are 'wasting' that peripheral vision on the margin. By making this simple change, our eyes only move about 75 per cent of the distance they did previously; we've just increased our speed by 25 per cent. Try reading a few pages like this now, to get the hang of it.

Use a tracker

Use a pen or your finger to track your reading. This prevents wasting time from losing your place and from 'back-reading', which is a tendency we all have to reread sections we've already read. You can lay a pen flat against the book or hold it as normal, as you prefer. Move the tracker across the words at a steady pace and follow it with your eyes – it might take a little practice to find a speed you are comfortable with.

Overclock

Just before you retest your speed, do the following exercise for three minutes. Use both of the techniques you've practised up to now but move your tracker very quickly. Go so fast that you cannot actually comprehend what you are reading – but do stay alert and try to keep up. Don't worry about comprehension at this point – this is just to 'overclock' your speed. This practice is similar in principle to baseball batters, who swing a very heavy bat just before they step up to the plate, so that when they swing a normally weighted one, they can swing it faster. Likewise, this exercise, if done before reading, will increase your speed temporarily.

After you've done that, go back to the start of this section and follow the instructions that gave you your baseline reading. Use the same book you tested your baseline with but use a section of the book you haven't read yet. Typically, people double their speed (based on my non-scientific observations).

Practise!

If your results are not as great as I suggest or if they are good but you feel your comprehension has suffered, then schedule some extra practice sessions. Use a book that you're not actively studying, to remove the pressure of having to be productive, and just use the time to practise these skills. Try using one at a time – start by not reading the whole line but go at your normal pace. After you've clocked up a few hours' doing this (over the space of several days), gradually increase your speed.

When you are actually studying, however, stay at a pace that allows you full comprehension, unless you are skimming. This is why I don't like the term speed reading very much – it implies 'rushed' reading but that's really not accurate. You still engage with the book – stop and think about what the author is trying to say, why it's important, whether you agree with it, how it connects with other theories, and so on – but when you are simply reading the words and sentences, you are doing it faster; and of course, speed reading really comes into its own on those earlier passes of the book, where you're selecting and rejecting the sections you'll need. By the way, we'll discuss how to engage with the material in depth on page 73.

With a little practice, these techniques – combined with the selective reading described earlier – will drastically increase your reading speed. Books that would normally take you several days to get through, you'll finish in an afternoon. That intimidating pile of 'books to read' will actually begin to shrink, instead of perpetually growing. Of course, if you want to read the rest of these books out of personal interest, you can still do so in your leisure time.

Effective note taking

I really think people have the wrong idea about note taking and it's mainly because we're never taught how to do it properly. Note taking generally is used to write down something that the lecturer says, so that you can reread or remember it later. In a sense, people view note taking as a kind of selective transcription. Perhaps this is what you do.

The idea of selecting the important points is correct but, overall, this approach is not effective. Note-taking should represent processing. A lecture should not be a passive listening experience; you should be listening and thinking as the lecturer speaks. You'll have to process the material at some point anyway; don't end up doing work later that you could have done in the lecture hall. Do as much thinking and reflecting as you can while sat there in the lecture. Don't just write down the facts, because you can get those from the lecture slides later. Instead, note down your thoughts, reflections, the implications, conclusions, the importance of what is being said. What does it mean?

Science is all about questions and answers. What are the underlying questions? What are the conclusions? What evidence supports these conclusions?

Cal Newport created this approach with his Q/E/C method (question/evidence/conclusion). You can read more about that and his other ideas at calnewport.com. The idea is to train yourself, while listening, to identify the question behind what the lecturer is saying and what is the answer (conclusion) to that question. Also take down all the supporting evidence for that conclusion, although in psychology the evidence is usually a reference and you can look up the references from the slides and your reading list. Therefore, your notes might look more like Q/A, with the question written in the margin or on the left side of the page and the answer written as a series of bullet points underneath or beside it.

I was sceptical about taking notes in this way, until I came to review the notes I'd taken after trying it. They were the best-organized notes I'd ever taken; very easy to read back through and pick up from where I left off. This method also forces processing during the lecture, rather than passive transcribing. Also, the practice of looking for the underlying question helps you to pick out the large themes and big ideas, which gives you a feel for the big picture. Thus, you create a deeper understanding of the material, rather then just learning surface facts.

Whether you use Q/E/C or Q/A, avoid taking notes verbatim. The natural note-taking instinct is to copy things from textbooks word for word or to furiously try to write down everything that a lecturer is saying. This isn't necessary most of the time. Try to write in keyword form rather than in full sentences. You won't remember full sentences anyway and it's easy to translate keywords into sentences when you need to. Notes should also be in bullets where possible, rather than writing full lines or paragraphs. Try to make your notes as easy to scan as possible, so it's easier to find what you need later and your pages of notes are not intimidating to look at. Using keywords and bullets also leaves plenty of 'white space' to add in extra notes, draw arrows between related points and other useful things.

Listen to your lectures and papers

Sometimes it can be hard to find the time to study, especially if you have commitments outside your course. But here is a way you can do potentially an extra 10–20 hours of study per week, without taking up any more of your spare time.

Buy yourself a Dictaphone and record your lectures and papers on to an MP3 player. Put them on your iPod or similar device and then listen to them as you commute, do chores, work out at the gym, and so on. I used to have a job that involved walking around London putting flyers on cars. I could do an extra seven hours of studying each night by listening to lectures and journal papers as I walked around. Maybe you can think of similar opportunities for yourself.

Some of your professors will record their lectures and make them available for you online but I recommend that you record your own anyway, just in case there are any technical glitches at their end.

As for the journal papers, there are two ways to listen to the written word. The first is to read your papers out loud into your recorder, for later listening. If you don't mind the sound of your own voice, this can be a good option for you. If you do mind the sound of your voice on tape, get a program for your computer that converts text files into your MP3 player. Many such programs are available for free online. I won't recommend a specific one, since the technology is improving quickly and my suggestion would quickly fall out of data. However, they can be found by Googling 'text to MP3 free' and similar phrases. The voices sound a little robotic but they are perfectly legible and rapidly getting better.

5   Keep the information in

If you've ever tried to learn a second language, you'll know how annoying it can be to try to keep new information in your head. You learn a new word and in that moment you're certain that you'll remember it. But ten minutes later, it's gone. When you first learn something, it sits in working memory and some of that information is then encoded for storage in long-term memory. Many things work against this process, such as memory decay and interference.

Therefore it is particularly important that we take steps to ensure that we remember what we learn: so that we can link it to future information and see how it all relates, recall it in exams, discuss it with others and generally impress people with how good our memory is. There's little point in understanding something if you don't remember it.

Luckily, there are many ways you can stack the memory deck in your favour. The ones we'll cover here are:

- memory skills
- revision schedule
- mind maps
- recall tests
- exercise.

Memory skills

A common theme through this book is that there is a disconnect between common study practice and what's most efficient. This is no more apparent than when it comes to memorizing what you learn. Based on my observations, this seems to be the general plan:

- Go to a lecture, take some notes.
- Do some further reading, make a few more notes.
- Do nothing until about one month before an exam.
- Dig out the notes, read through them a few times and perhaps copy them out on to a new page.

This is a highly inefficient way to remember things!

You would think that study skills in psychology courses would counter this by developing skills that take into account all that cognitive psychology has to teach us about memory. But alas, the tyranny of outdated study skills prevails. In the pages ahead, I'll show you how to make memorising easy, and the best part is that you don't need to be a memory master to receive benefits. I myself only had a basic grasp of these methods while at university but had no problem recalling information in exams.

Before we look at some specific techniques, let's address a common criticism of memory skills in studying. Some people point out that your course isn't about merely memorizing things and regurgitating them in the exams, and that you will get a low grade if you do this. I agree. There's little point in remembering something if you don't understand it. You will definitely need to understand and form your own position on the material and there is more on that on page 75. Having said that, it's a simple truth that unless your course does not involve exams, your ability to recall a large number of facts will be tested at some point in the future; you cannot avoid this. It's also a simple truth that there are easy ways and hard ways to remember things. Why not find the easy ways?

Baseline measurement

As with the speed-reading exercises, don't just take my word that these techniques work. Let's get a baseline measurement first of all. Spend three minutes looking over the list of words in the box below and later in the chapter I'll ask you to recall the words. Keep a pen and paper at the ready for when I do. After that, I'll give another list of words, which you'll memorize using some of the techniques you are about to learn. Then we'll see if there has been an improvement.

Cat	Toast
Shoe	Mouse
Wall	Leaf
Car	Ball
Cloud	Paint

The link system

Now that you've had a go at memorizing a list of words, we'll look at the two main memory techniques. The first one is the link system. This is a classic memory technique, one that magicians use to memorize massive lists of words. It is not an intuitive way of thinking, so it will take a little bit of practice to do this effectively; but with less than an hour's practice, you'll probably be stunned at how much your memory has improved.

The link system uses creative visualization of words to aid their recall at a later time. The traditional way of explaining this is to use the example of a shopping list. Say you are going shopping and want to memorize the words 'carrot', 'chicken' and 'flowers' so you don't forget these items. You would create a visualization that integrates these words, two at a time. The key to the link system is to make the visualizations absolutely, completely, absurdly, ridiculous. The more outlandish and crazy they are, the more they will stand out in your mind.

So first you might link carrot and chicken, by visualising a number of giant carrots, with a beaks and wings, walking around a farm. They are three feet tall and occasionally peck at the ground. This is a good example of the level of silliness you should aim for. Hold the image in your mind for a few seconds and you're done.

To continue linking a list of words, you drop the first one and then link the third word to the second. The next item on our shopping list was flowers, so we could imagine a prince approaching a princess, dropping to one knee and handing her a bunch of chickens. You get the idea. Make the image big and silly and hold it in your mind for a few seconds. If we had a longer list, we'd link the next item to 'flowers' and repeat the process to the end of the list.

The memory palace

Also called the method of loci, the second memory technique uses spatial associations to trigger memories. This is what the memory masters often use when memorizing the order of multiple decks of cards and other incredible feats. Luckily, it's quite easy to learn. The principle of the system is to memorize a 'memory palace', which is a mental journey around an environment you are very familiar with. At various point around the journey, you identify 'pegs', on to which you 'hook' different things that you want to remember, using the link system.

For example, when I was at university my palace started in my room and the first peg was my bedroom door. I walked out of my room and my flatmate was stood in the doorway to his room. That's peg 2. At the top of the stairs was a mirror; that's peg 3. You get the idea.

The first step is to figure out what your palace will be and what the pegs will be. It must be a journey rather than a static image and you need to strongly ingrain your palace into your memory. If possible, try to physically walk the journey, noting the pegs as you go. If you cannot physically walk the journey, walk it mentally. Do this several times. Also, write your list of pegs down and use the link system to commit them to memory.

If you have got the hang of the link system, the memory palace will be simple. Just use your crazy visualisation in the same way as before but link the thing you want to remember to each peg on the journey. Mentally walk the journey and associate as you go. So, for our shopping list, I might imagine that instead of a bedroom door, there is a man dressed in a huge carrot costume and he's stood munching on a raw carrot. I have to struggle to squeeze past big carrot man and get out of my room. When I do, I see my flatmate in a violent fistfight with a giant chicken. And so on.

The palace has many advantages over the link system. With the link, if you forget one point in the chain you might end up losing everything that came after it. With the palace, you can go to any point in your journey and then work backwards or forwards from there. You just have to ensure that the journey is completely memorized – take some time out to make sure you have done so.

These memory tricks are simple to learn but they do take a little practice to get down. By putting in a little learning up-front, you'll save yourself time in the future.

How to apply the techniques

These techniques are specifically designed for recall. It is not necessary to use this for every thing you learn, as a way of filing information away – only things you'll specifically need to recall. So, naturally, where these methods really come into their own is in exams. If you've read the section on note taking, your notes should be keyword heavy, rather than predominantly in full sentences. This is completely compatible with the link system. If you have a list of keywords prepared for an exam, you can use the link system to remember them.

You could memorize a list of the major researchers, which could jog your memory about their work, ideas, specific papers, etc. You might have to pick out a section of their name to use in the link, for example for 'Clifton' you might visualize a cliff face, for 'Shaw' a shoreline, and so on. If the name does not have an obvious image, try to think of a celebrity or sports personality with the same name and visualize them. If there are a few key papers you will need for an exam, use the link system to memorize them. You'll have to devise a keyword for each one that will remind you about that paper and link these keywords together.

Using this technique, along with the mind map ideas below, it's possible to memorize several full essay plans, so you can have a few answers prepared for likely questions that might come up (but don't rely solely on this! See the section on preparing for exams on page 114).

Where these ideas fall a little short, however, is in complex concepts and broad ideas, for which they are not really suitable – unless you can break them down into a list of words representing different aspects of the theory in question (which might be a useful exercise in itself).

Above all, if you use these methods, make sure you go over your links and palaces occasionally to cement them in memory (include them in your revision schedule, which we'll discuss on the next page).

OK, grab your paper and pen and try to write down as many as you can of the ten words you were presented with earlier. Don't cheat! Give yourself a couple of minutes, starting now.

. . .

How did you do? Given the interference of the sections you've been reading and assuming you have no prior training in memory techniques, I'd say that you probably remembered five or fewer. More than that and your memory is already pretty good, in my opinion.

Let's try again, this time use the link system. Go back to page 64 and review the instructions – remember, big, silly, ridiculous images, and hold them in your mind for a few seconds. Try again with the list below and, later in the chapter I'll test you again.

Tree	Ring
Shop	Sun
Phone	Web
Dog	Table
Book	Hat

Revision scheduling

For this tip you will need a diary – preferably an academic one that runs from September to September – and a pen.

We need to rethink the crazy idea of learning topics only once through the year, forgetting it as we move on to other topics and then doing 2–3 weeks of revision at the end when we try to remember everything. I found it insanely difficult to learn this way and, judging by the overall stress level around campus at exam time, so did everyone else.

Revision should be an ongoing process, not a cram session, so start a revision schedule immediately. Take your academic diary and, when you've finished studying each day, schedule in revision sessions for what you learned at the following intervals:

- ten minutes later
- 24 hours later
- one week later
- one month later
- six months later.

These are the intervals that allegedly give you the best shot at 'permanently' remembering, without overloading you with revision. In my experience, it is not permanent but it certainly is effective for a year to get you through your exams.

A review session is quite a simple activity. It might involve:

- Jotting down, as a keyword list or in a mind map, anything you can remember about the topic.
- Reading through your notes and reviewing your mind maps.
- If you've made any recall tests or flashcards (see page 70), you can use them here too.
- If you can't access your notes, paper or a pen for some reason, try to at least spend some time thinking about the topic and seeing what you can recall about it.

The first review ten minutes after you finish studying is arguably the most important. It is thought that a little revision here triggers your brain to encode the information to long-term memory. Never just close your books and switch the TV on – wherever possible, do a review session of what you have just done.

In fact, you should do the same thing after each of your lectures. Go to the library or other quiet area, and spend five to ten minutes going over the lecture you just had. What were the main themes? What were you not clear on? What were the major questions and conclusions of the research you learned about? Read through any notes you made. You will probably resist doing this at first, but a little effort here will save you from relearning all the things you'll forget if you didn't do this.

I also recommend reviewing the new things you have learned each day before you go to bed; it is thought that this can help retain the information, particularly if you dream about it.

To schedule the future review sessions, just put a note at the above time points in your diary to indicate the topics you'll review that day. Check your diary each day; make this the first thing you do each time you sit down to study. You don't need to spend a lot of time reviewing. Three minutes is fine, five minutes if you're feeling particularly motivated. If you have a lot to review on the same day, limit the overall review session to 20 minutes. Don't make this too much of a chore and you'll be more likely to keep it up.

Reviewing is a nice easy task and it can get you sat down at your desk quite well. If you think you've got a big essay to work on, for instance, the sheer size of the task can prevent you from even getting started. Reviewing is a good way to get sat down and into the flow of studying and, once you're there, suddenly that essay is not quite as intimidating any more.

Mind maps

I highly recommend creating mind maps for all topics you will be taking exams on. By 'mind map', I'm referring to the full-on, illustrated, A3-size, technicolour version. Here's why: the average page of notes, when written by people who haven't been taught effective note-taking methods, is a block of text. Maybe it's split into paragraphs, maybe not. I used to write full pages of notes without paragraphs or indents. Maybe the odd heading here and there but that's about it.

Better notes are in bullet format, as described on page 60. This is much better, to be sure, but note taking is primarily a method of capturing information. Even if your notes are beautifully arranged, they all look pretty much the same as each other. There's nothing to distinguish one page from any other.

The same cannot be said of mind maps. Go to Google Images (images.google.com) and search for 'mind map'. There's just no comparison is there? Mind maps stand out much more; they're more memorable in every way. Because of this, when you're in an exam and you need to jog your memory, you'll find it easier to visualize your mind map than a page of notes. You've written hundreds of pages of notes and they all look the same. Mind maps are unique.

Tony Buzan's *The mind map book* has detailed instructions on how to use mind maps. Check if your library has it or something similar. In the mean time, you can get a basic idea by looking at the Google results. You'll see some great examples of how it's done (although ignore the computer-generated ones). When drawing your own, observe the following rules:

- The centre of the map should be an image of some kind.
- Use A3 paper or larger (A4 is too small).
- Each branch should be a different colour.
- Where you can, draw images around the map, related to things nearby.
- Branches should start fairly thick and get thinner as they move outwards.
- Write the words along the branches – not at the point the branches point to.
- Use keywords as much as possible – avoid sentences.

Much like the memory techniques described earlier, you are making the information more memorable by varying a number of different modalities throughout the map. When you are in an exam – or any time you need to recall information on the topic – you can ask yourself the following questions:

- What was my central picture?
- How many branches came out of the centre and what did they represent?
- What was on the red/green/blue/whatever branches?
- What was in the top left? Top right? etc.
- What images did I draw? What did they represent? What was near them?

In effect, you have set up a large number of memory triggers for the material. Plus, you get the usual benefits of laying ideas out in this way – they are organized in a way that makes sense to you, it's easier to link different ideas together, it's all on one page, etc.

Pin your mind maps up on your wall and review them occasionally throughout the year. When it gets closer to exam time (within two weeks), try to recreate the mind map from memory (roughly that is; not in colour), to see where the gaps in your recall are. Focus extra effort on these areas – going over things you can already recall is a waste of time. As you learn other topics, you'll find that some things relate to what you've already put on a mind map. At this point you can add the new information to the map. By the way, don't worry if it looks out of place – a mind map is a tool for learning, not a piece of art.

Before we move on to recall tests as another learning tool, let's do a recall test right now. If you haven't read the previous section on memory techniques yet, you can skip this bit. Grab your paper and pen and try to write down as many as you can of the ten words you were presented with in the second list – the one on which you practised the link system. Give yourself a couple of minutes, starting now.

. . .

Much better, eh? I'll bet you got all ten words. If you didn't, don't worry, just practise the techniques a little more and try again (use a free online random word generator to come up with new words if you wish). Do a little postmortem analysis of your images – were they outrageous, silly, out of the ordinary? The closer they are to 'real' life, the more they will blend into the million other similar memories you have. Make sure they stand out!

Recall tests

A fantastic way to learn a subject in great depth is to regularly test your recall. As you come across something you will need to remember, form a question around it and write it down somewhere. If you've used the question/evidence/conclusion or the question/answer method of note taking described earlier, you're ready to go almost straight away. I prefer to use text files on the computer, because I can type much faster than I can write and I can search for the file and open it without even moving my hands off the keyboard (on the Mac, Command + Spacebar opens up Spotlight/Searchlight), on Windows 7, press the Windows key).

Put the answers to the questions on a separate sheet of paper or on the back if you can't see through it. If it's a text file, hold return down for a few seconds and leave a huge gap. Your review sessions are a great time to pull out your recall tests but anytime is a good time to do some recall tests on areas that feel a little 'hazy' – especially the topics you know you'll have exams on.

Flashcards

I wish I had known about flashcards while I was at university! The method is simple but hugely effective. Get yourself some index cards from a stationery shop. Make sure they are thick enough that what you write won't show through on the other side. On one side of the flashcard, write a question. On the other side, write the answer. This is better for those little facts that you have to memorize but, if you can fit a few keywords on the index card, it'll be useful for all questions. Here's an example:

Side 1:
Traits in the five-factor model?

Side 2:
Openness to experience
Conscientiousness
Extraversion
Agreeableness
Neuroticism

There's a specific way to test yourself with a flashcards: give yourself only around ten seconds of thinking time. If you think for 11 seconds and then get the correct answer, that's classed as incorrect. In cases like the above example, feel free to give yourself more time, as there are technically five answers you have to give.

When you get a question right, put the flashcard on the right side of your desk, or in your right pocket if you're on the move (you can take your flashcards anywhere with you). If you get a question wrong or have to think too hard about it, it goes in the left pocket. Go through the deck until you get to the end, and then take all the cards out of your left pocket and repeat.

If you know the answer to a question within ten seconds, there's no point in going over it again for a while. The benefits of 'over-learning' tail off sharply and the return on investment is not worth the time. So it's better to spend as much time as possible on the areas you are less sure of, and flashcards are a great way to make sure you do that. Eventually, you'll have a solid ability to recall what was on the cards and, if you do this while commuting, it won't take up any more of your spare time, either.

6 Understand the information

During my first degree, I noticed two kinds of students. One kind really tried to understand and attack the theories and ideas. They usually sat near the front or the middle and asked a lot of questions in lectures. The second kind did not try to understand psychology but tried to 'get through' their course. They usually sat at the back, rarely asked questions and – I'm not joking – would sometimes listen to their iPods throughout the lecture.

Guess who got the best grades? Guess who had the least stress at exam time? I remember one girl, standing outside the exam hall, smiling, relaxed, as if she was waiting to see a show or something. At the time I thought she was either crazy or in the wrong place; now I know she just fell into the first category of student.

As I'll keep saying, it is not sufficient to memorize information and spit it back out it in an exam. Not if you want a decent grade anyway. There's this idea that the sciences are all about the memorization and regurgitation of information, and that is simply not the case. As well as getting your facts right, you'll also need to 'show your understanding' and use 'critical thinking' as you 'engage with the material.' But what do these strange things actually mean?

Essentially, they mean that there is a difference between memorizing information and understanding broad concepts. You should identify the big concepts and understand how they relate to each other (or not). You should also be familiar with the evidence that supports these concepts and have conducted your own critical inspection of this evidence. So, in psychology, we could say that 'understanding' involves two things: *concepts* and *evidence*. It is not enough to demonstrate that you possess knowledge of these things but, rather, you must demonstrate your processing of these things. In other words, show you have developed and applied cognitive skills to analyze, criticize, synthesize and evaluate. In short:

- don't get any facts wrong
- demonstrate that you have processed the material
- show how the big concepts relate to each other
- give a critical analysis of the evidence for them.

What is evidence?

We've discussed the nature of evidence in depth in previous chapters. It is the data onto which the theories rest – the legs of the table (see page 8).

What are concepts?

By 'concepts', I mean the theories, themes and frameworks into which all the little facts fit. It's the bigger picture. Sometimes a particular concept will be explicit (e.g., evolution by natural selection), sometimes you'll notice your own themes and patterns by pulling different theories together. We discussed ways to 'pry' out big ideas when taking notes by using Cal Newport's question/evidence/conclusion method or the simplified question/answer version. As you're reading a paper or listening to a lecture, ask yourself, 'What is the underlying question behind this information?'. This helps you identify the concepts.

The rest of this chapter is organized into two sections. The first is devoted to showing you a few ways in which you can develop your understanding of the material you are being presented with – how to get your head around it and feel comfortable with it. The second focuses on criticism – how to evaluate the strength of the supporting evidence.

Both of these aspects – understanding and criticizing – are essential to doing well in the course.

Developing your understanding of concepts

We've discussed ways to locate information. We know how to read quickly and effectively. We've learned techniques to help us keep the information in our heads. What happens when we read something we need to know and we don't understand it? What if it just goes right over our heads?

How to deal with difficult material

Slow down! As I've said previously, don't worry about reading quickly when you're trying to understand a topic. Go back over the material again, slowly. Pause and reflect frequently and try to explain to yourself what you have just read (either out loud or in your head, as you prefer). Then continue. Doing this will help you to highlight which specific parts you are struggling with.

It can also help to read the paper out loud. When we start reading material that's pretty tough going, we need to engage and focus more. Unfortunately, the opposite tends to happen and our brains drift off. Have you ever noticed that you daydream more often while reading difficult material? One way to minimize this is to read out loud.

If you are still having trouble, move on to a different topic. Let what you have taken in so far incubate in your mind and come back to it later. You might well find the material far easier to get through this way than by stressing yourself out by struggling with difficult areas. There's a common perception that studying has to be really hard and that, if you don't hate it, you're not doing it right. Well this isn't true and stress isn't going to help you. If you are struggling, take a break and when you come back, move on to something else. Let it incubate a while.

If you're still stuck, ask; talk to your lecturer (tips on this ahead) or ask your classmates. Whatever you do, don't gloss over something you don't understand, never to return to it – fill in your knowledge gap now. If you don't, you'll only have to deal with it at a more stressful time (i.e., close to your exams). You don't want to be learning new things during exam time, only reviewing what you have learned.

To summarize these points on dealing with difficult material:

- Reread the material.
- Read slowly, pause to reflect often.
- Read it out loud.
- Let it incubate for a while and come back to it.

Increase your understanding by crossing disciplines

When thinking about psychological theories, don't limit yourself to the specific subdiscipline that your class is teaching. Think about how the theories relate to those in other areas. Are they compatible? Do any theories contradict it? This can not only help you to understand the material by looking at it through a different lens but, in addition, linking in work from other areas is a great way to score those coveted 'wide reading' marks in your assignments and essays.

Evolutionary theories are worth a particular mention here. Because they seek to explain behaviour on a different level ('ultimate' rather than 'proximate' explanations – look it up), it is usually possible to look at almost all areas of psychology from an evolutionary perspective.

Similarly, cognitive psychology and neuroscience look at the cognitive processes that we all share. So, because there is a part of the brain controlling all of our behaviours, you can look at any behaviour from the perspective of the behaviour itself, the cognitive processes that produce it, the brain areas associated with these processes and the evolutionary reasons that such a cognitive process would exist.

Remember to check your ideas out against research and, if you are speculating, make sure you know you are doing so. In an essay you might even say something like 'It could be argued that x evolved to solve the problem of y, although further research is needed to test this hypothesis . . .' where 'y' would be an area of debate in evolutionary psychology. If you have space, you could even briefly describe the specific study that would need to be done.

Here's an example. Take belief bias: the tendency for people to forgo logic when it contradicts their existing beliefs. Cognitive psychologists explain that this is due to the dual processing model of reasoning. We have one system that is fast and relies on 'rules of thumb' and another that is slower and uses conscious reasoning. Unless we specifically activate the conscious system, the automatic one will give us a quick answer, which, although it might not be accurate, has served us well in the past. Evolutionary theorists might argue that different problems in similar environments are also likely to be similar and fast reaction times might be the difference between life and death; hence, the automatic system usually gets first shot at producing an output behaviour.

Here you have a few different ways of looking at the same behaviour, all compatible, and these different perspectives help you to understand the big idea better. I've mentioned evolutionary and cognitive/neuroscience theories because they are popular and arguably the easiest disciplines to cross into but use whatever you like and know. If you are unfamiliar with evolution, try something else. What would behaviourists make of belief bias, or social constructionists, or humanists?

Crossing disciplines is especially useful when two disciplines or theories contradict each other. Some theories have a harder time dealing with certain evidential findings than others. Remember the process of science we talked about earlier? The aim of the game is to build these theoretical models that account for the findings of the research. Sometimes different theories are quite compatible but, more often, theories are in contrast and to synthesize them will need some 'tweaking'. Can you think of any theories that oppose the one you are studying?

Maybe the two theories can be reconciled, maybe not. For instance, perhaps they are both correct under different conditions. How could you find this out? Try to shape your inquiry into a question you can pursue and follow your line of thought. Don't worry about getting a definitive answer though; that's the job of future research. What you can do is understand that there is a contradiction and think up ideas for future studies that might help to investigate the two opposing theories.

Even if you can't get to a satisfactory answer (I have no idea what humanistic theories would make of belief bias), doing the mental gymnastics will help you understand the information and therefore you'll recall it more easily because of this. This is studying.

Study groups

If you can find a group of people you like who are sincerely interested in the topics, it can be a great idea to form a study group. You could meet to discuss things from the classes you all have in common. Anything you have a firm grasp of, you can explain to them, and what they know well, they will explain to you.

Be selective when forming a study group. Be like George Clooney in *Ocean's 11*; pick the best people you can get. However, two to four people is probably best unless you know each other well.

You'll have to find a good frequency too. I think once a week is a good frequency. Too often and attendance/commitment might drop off and less often might not be as effective as you would like. However, go with whatever works for you. You should also find a suitable location you can use – see if you can book a room at your university for this purpose.

Study groups will help you by 'forcing' you to express your thoughts verbally to other people and by processing what other people have to say. The active element of discussion will give you far greater ability to recall the material than just reading in your head or rewriting notes.

Do try to keep the group focused though. It can be tempting to talk about the latest episode of *whatever-you-watch* or that night out where you had 13 shots of tequila and woke up in a dustbin (OK maybe that's just me), but save this for after the study session. Have clear start and end points to the meeting and know what you will be covering before you start the session. Otherwise, you'll waste too much time deciding what to do. You can organize all this by mailing everyone as a group.

Mentoring

Finding a mentor might be a great idea and is certainly worth looking into. But I had something else in mind here. It is said that surgeons are trained by the principle of 'Watch one, do one, teach one', and I think there's a lot be said for the idea of learning by teaching. It takes a different sort of processing to explain something to someone else, because although you might feel like you have a grasp of something, that can change once you try to put it into words!

Helping students in lower years might also give you some confidence. You are filling the role of 'tutor' and knowing that other people view you as a fountain of knowledge may help you to view yourself in that way too. However, be aware that the topics you'll cover with your mentee may not be totally compatible with what you are studying now – so consider the time/benefit balance carefully.

Thinking on paper

It can be very useful to take some time out to just write about the topic you are studying, particularly when there is a problem or issue you are struggling with. If you are writing an essay and come across a difficult problem, it can be tempting to use the essay paper as your canvas for working on the problem. However, it's better to do this elsewhere, because when you have loaded up essay.doc you are in 'essay writing mode', not 'understand the subject mode'. You'll try to write in essay style – you are writing for someone else other than yourself, you'll parse yourself, try to make your points logically flow and so on; all of which limits your creative thinking significantly.

So load up another blank document and use this as your sketch pad. Or, if you prefer, go analogue and get a paper and pen. Your Facebook account and email don't tempt you when you're writing in a notebook. If you live in a warm climate you could even go outside, to the park or the beach. There's no rule that says studying has to be done inside the library or your house; if anything, novel environments might trigger your brain to think in new ways.

Here are two ways to think on paper:

1. *Use your notepad to summarize ideas in your own words*. This might seem like a daunting task because, if any concepts aren't clear to you, this will become quite

apparent! However, this is a good thing; it highlights the gaps in your knowledge and the areas to research further. This idea is similar in principle to recall tests – except you are testing free recall rather than being prompted by a question.

2. *Think on paper about a specific problem or area you don't understand.* Don't necessarily do this with the aim of finding the 'right answer'. The simple process of thinking deeply about the topic, coming up with ideas, and so on, is the desired end result you are looking for here. This is basically a crutch to help you do the necessary mental processing. I made many a 'breakthrough' in my own understanding by doing this.

Ask for help

Sometimes, even after a lot of hard work, you'll still struggle with something. This is completely fine! If your recommended readings, notes and thinking have not given you the understanding you want, seek further help from your lecturer. Go to them with the specific problem you are having and make sure to point out the bits you already do understand. If you haven't even tried to study a particular concept, don't go to the lecturer. What would you expect them to do in that case? Give you the lecture again right there?

No, that would give completely the wrong impression. Show your lecturers that you are putting hard work and effort into your studies – be active in lectures, ask questions and, if you go to them for further clarification, make it known that you are working on this and just need a little extra help. There are practical reasons for this. If you put in a piece of work that's veering on the edge of a decent grade, the marker's knowledge of how hard you are working might push your grade in the right direction.

Criticizing theory

When we talk about criticism in science, it's not the same as in films or restaurants. It isn't the time to sound off your opinions in a persuasive and flamboyant manner. Criticism is meant to be a constructive appraisal of a piece of work. As we've already seen, research is never perfect, so we have to make sure we are aware of the limitations of the data we're drawing our theories from. When being critical, we can either be critical of the theory itself, or critical of the evidence.

Criticizing the theory itself

The following tips apply mainly to theories and theory papers – those that don't necessarily report any new research (or sometimes they will propose a new theory alongside one or more studies in the same paper) but the main purpose of the paper is to describe a new theory. Ideally, their arguments will be supported by evidence but sometimes researchers will essentially propose a hypothesis, often as a call for other labs to research it too. Another type of theory paper is the critique, where a researcher will write up his concerns over a particular theory, his reasoning and his own interpretation, if relevant. In this case, you'll have to critique the critique. As well as these cases, this section also applies to the introduction and discussion sections of research papers.

Just a quick reminder before we go on; as well as the information here, I recommend that you get yourself a good book on critical reasoning. Any that your library has available will be good and I hope you have already got your hands on Stanovich's (2009) excellent *How to think straight about psychology*.

The value of a theory

When criticizing a theory, think of it in terms of its usefulness in bringing us towards a stronger understanding of the phenomena it explains. A theory is valuable if it accurately reflects the world 'out there'. We can be fairly sure it reflects the world out there when there is a large amount of evidence supporting it. We'll look at evidence soon but, first, just because there is evidence does not necessarily make the theory correct as it is. There may be alternative theories that can account for the same or perhaps more evidence. There may be evidence that the theory is unable to account for, that the authors have neglected to consider for some reason. The following principles and questions will help you analyze the value of a theory.

Comprehensiveness

Theories all differ in their breadth (the range of topics they cover) and their depth (how many hypotheses are drawn from it about a particular topic and how specific these hypotheses are).

Accuracy

A theory is given more weight when a greater number of its hypotheses have been supported by empirical research. We'll cover evidence later but another point to keep in mind is falsifiability. You might remember this from page 9; it refers to whether testable hypotheses can be drawn from the theory. If a testable hypothesis cannot be derived from the theory, it is useless; or at least, not scientific.

If there are empirical data for a particular phenomenon that the theory would not predict, we have a little problem. New theories need to account for all the facts that have been previously observed and documented. Either the theory needs to be modified or the research was poorly conducted and does not reflect reality.

Parsimony

Is the theory overly complex? In science, the simplest explanation wins the day. For example, we have studied biological processes in plants and understand how they grow and reproduce. So, if someone proposes the theory that God or some spiritual energy controls life, these aspects are, in a sense, dead weight to our model. We already have a physical explanation, so we don't need to add on another concept to explain what we have observed. As long as all the relevant research can be accounted for, theories are better when they are more parsimonious.

Critical questions

To help you uncover flaws in any argument, ask the following questions of it (this is not specific to psychology papers, but any written argument):

- *Are the arguments consistent throughout?* Look out for contradictions.
- *Is there evidence of bias?* Does the author seem to favour one position without a balanced discussion of alternatives?
- *Are all the arguments relevant?* In particular, look out for 'straw men'. Sometimes an argument will be proposed that appears to be an argument against an opposing position but in fact, is not. However, many readers will mentally score a point in the writer's favour nonetheless. For example, say we're talking about evolution, and you say 'You believe that since we're programmed to survive we must all be evil and vicious but I've seen many kind acts in my day, so evolution cannot be true'. Anyone listening may think 'I've seen kind acts too . . . he's right!' but, of course, I never held the position that all people are vicious in the first place. This is the 'straw man' argument – creating a straw man that is easier to knock down than the opponent's true position. It's a dirty trick and it is used when people want to win arguments rather than work towards the truth.
- *Are there any assumptions in the arguments that have not been backed up by logic or empirical evidence?* Look out for underlying assumptions that have not been backed up. Any theory built on them will collapse like a house of cards if that assumption turns out not to be true. Likewise, be wary of explicitly unsupported arguments.
- *Does it cover the history of and demonstrate reasonable development of converging evidence?* Or is the supporting evidence limited to a particular variety or time period?
- *Is it well balanced – has it excluded any relevant research that you know about?* You may remember that even meticulously conducted science will throw up a few false results once in a while and science conducted poorly will do so more often. So it's possible to 'cherry pick' only the evidence that supports a position and ignore the rest. To the reader who does not know about the rest of the evidence, it may seem like a strong case. The whole body of evidence must be considered.
- *Are any of the basic premises founded on non peer-reviewed material?* I read a health website that seemed very scientific, including reference lists. I was initially impressed, until I looked more closely and saw that they were referencing Wikipedia and Ezine articles – what's to stop the authors writing for these sites and then referencing themselves, to give the appearance of credibility? Peer-review is not perfect but it does help to separate the wheat from the chaff.
- *Is it treating anecdotal evidence as scientific?* This is more common outside of science but you should still be aware of it at all times. Case studies, testimonials and anecdotes

are not scientific. They might inform future studies but they are not sufficient in themselves. Many media scare stories are based on anecdotes disguised as science – look up the MMR (measles, mumps and rubella) scare in the UK for a good example.

- *Has the theory been widely tested?* We talked earlier about the fact that one study, even if immaculately conducted, is not enough. The theory has to be tested by different researchers in different situations to really identify its strengths and weaknesses. If the evidence is too 'narrow', the theory may need further studies to justify the arguments.
- *Have other papers published since countered or adjusted it?* Scientific theories adapt and change over time. If you're looking at a paper from 1987, maybe the theory has been adjusted in light of new evidence since then. Look up more recent papers to make sure you know what the situation is.
- *Are there any exceptions to the arguments proposed?* Look for alternative explanations and exceptions to the 'rules' presented by the theory. If the theory proposes that 'x' is correct, can you think of any times, places or examples in which 'x' is not correct?
- *Is the evidence relevant to the point being made?* Be sure to look up the papers in support of an argument, particularly where it is critical to a paper you are writing or your own lines of inquiry around a subject. Just because you see a set of brackets and a year, this does not tick the 'supported' box. The study may be poor quality or may be completely unrelated to the actual argument (I've seen this, believe it or not).
- *Is there enough evidence to support the point being made?* Another great quote: 'Extraordinary claims require extraordinary evidence'. This is true, much to the dismay of many wannabe psychics. The further away the point is from currently accepted and evidenced models of the world, the stronger the evidence required to support that point. This doesn't mean that a single study in support of an extraordinary claim should be dismissed immediately, it just means it will take more than that to justify modifying the theory.
- *Is the evidence strong enough to support the point being made?* In other words, does it have any flaws in method or analysis? Has the author interpreted any statistical data correctly?

The above questions, along with your further reading, will serve you well when it comes to critically analyzing theoretical models in psychology. But, as we see in the final point, we also have to look at the empirical evidence in support of theoretical arguments. This means spotting flaws in methodology and use of statistics, which gives us an understanding of the strength of the evidence.

Criticizing evidence

If you read a particular theory and understand it well but do not check the evidence behind it, you are practically taking the researchers' word for it. Of course, you might be aware that certain studies have been replicated, the researchers are highly regarded and have faith in the peer-review system; and these are all good things. They are there to help us to keep from believing something without good reason. But there is no place for authority in the sciences; no one gets an easy ride because they are a big name in the field – theories are accepted and rejected based on the data that support them and nothing else.

This is why psychology courses place such a high emphasis on critical thinking. If you are going to be a carpenter, you need to know about wood; what is good quality and what is poor. What's the point of having an elaborate design for a cabinet if it's made from poor-quality wood? It's liable to fall apart before too long or maybe it isn't strong enough to hold the weight of the items within it.

It's the same thing with evidence. If you're going to be a psychologist, you need to understand evidence. Why build a theory around poor quality evidence? It's liable to fall apart if a good-quality study contradicts it.

Sometimes the 'cabinets' in psychology are actually made of poor-quality wood, despite the safeguards. Other times, the cabinet is currently being worked on and over time the cheap plywood will be replaced with beautiful mahogany – maybe changing the design a little here and there to fit the new pieces in. So just because a cabinet (theory) exists, don't assume it's made of good quality wood (evidence). Maybe it's a work in progress, maybe it's just weak.

That said, some cabinets are incredibly well built and have stood the test of time and you can more or less accept them as fact (or as close to fact as science allows). The theory of evolution is a great example. But, naturally, the *amount* of evidence behind a theory will guide you, as well as the *quality* of that evidence.

How strong is the cabinet?

A lot of psychology students (especially those without any background in science) do not feel comfortable about critically analyzing research. They feel like they are not qualified. However, you are qualified. Anyone can grab a hammer and start knocking the different parts of a cabinet, to see if there are any weak points. As your critical thinking skills develop, your hammer will get bigger and stronger and you'll be able to see weak points in cabinets that previously seemed very strong. You'll get better and feel more confident with time but you've got to learn by doing. Hey, the cabinet analogy is pretty good, isn't it? I don't know where I get these ideas sometimes.

What to look out for when criticizing evidence

First things first; you have read the chapters on research methods and statistics, haven't you? And/or you've put extra effort into getting a stronger grasp of this from more dedicated sources?

The early chapters of this book plus your further study will put you in a strong position to evaluate the quality of evidence. The following questions will help you as a reference of things to look out for. I'm sure it's not exhaustive, so use it as a guide but don't rely on it entirely (the same applies to the critical questions above).

The subjects/participants

- Is the sample size adequate? i.e. at least 30 per group, preferably at least 50?
- Is the sample appropriate? How was it sourced? Is it yet another study on undergraduate psych students? Does that matter in this case?
- Is the sample too specific? A random sample from the population is not always needed but you should decide whether there are any psychological differences between the group being studied and the population at large that might make the results less generalizable.
- Is there any potential selection bias in the sample?
- What is the cultural mix? Is it biased towards a particular ethic, socio-economic, age or other demographic? If so, might the results be specific to this demographic or could they apply to others?
- Is there information available on the dropouts? If the dropout rate is high, what might this mean?

The Methodology

- What type of study was done? Was it an experiment, a quasi-experiment, a cross-sectional, naturalistic observation? Does the study design specifically tackle the hypothesis?
- Does the design of the study allow causality to be determined?
- Are the independent and dependent variables to be measured appropriate for the hypothesis?
- What could confounding factors/variables be and how are these addressed?
- How repeatable is the study?
- How was the assignment to groups performed? Was random assignment used and, if so, how was it done? Is there any potential for bias in group assignment?
- If possible, was assessment 'blind' or 'double-blind'?
- Is the placebo effect factored for? Has an adequate control condition been employed?

Measurement

- Are the concepts grounded on observable, measurable factors? You cannot test that which you cannot measure.
- Have the questionnaires and other measurements used been demonstrated in previous studies to measure what they are supposed to? In other words, do the measurements have high validity?
- Are the measurements reliable (high test–retest correlation)?
- Are they widely used or relatively new?

Analysis

- Have appropriate statistical procedures been used? Have they been used properly?
- Have the prerequisite conditions for those statistical procedures been met? (See your statistics textbooks for more information on these conditions.)
- Have any uncommon statistical tests been conducted and, if so, have they been sufficiently justified?
- Are the results statistically significant? Is the p value lower than .05?
- Has the effect size been reported? If so, is it large enough to be meaningful (minimum 0.2 for Cohen's d and .1 for r)?

Discussion

- Is there any confusion of causality and correlation? Has causality been assumed inappropriately (e.g., in a correlational design)?
- Has absence of evidence been treated as evidence of absence?
- Have the limitations of the study been properly highlighted?

Conclusions

- What are the main conclusions of the paper and does the evidence support them?
- Are there any other alternative interpretations that can be made of the results? Don't rely on what the authors say about the data – look at the numbers and draw your own conclusion. Are they right?
- Why are these conclusions important? Do they advance our knowledge, replicate a study or refute an existing theory?

The FiLCHeRS method of criticizing evidential arguments

FiLCHeRS is an acronym coined by James Lett (Lett, 1990) representing six rules of evidential reasoning. Each letter except the vowels represents one rule, so it's easy to remember and it's also comprehensive. Apply these principles to a few pseudoscientific claims – psychic powers, homeopathy, crystal healing – and then to some established scientific theories and note the differences.

   Note: *if a claim adheres to all these rules, it is not automatically correct! It is just more likely to be so.*

Falsifiability

We covered falsifiability on page 88. If a claim is so vague that a hypothesis cannot be drawn based on it, or if the claim is structured such that there no conceivable evidence would be satisfactory to disprove it, then it is unfalsifiable and therefore untestable.

Logic

Keep an eye out for arguments that are logically sound but based on incorrect assumptions. Likewise, look out for 'leaps' of logic, where the premises are correct but the conclusions do not follow from the premises. The critical reasoning books in any library will explain logic in more depth.

Comprehensiveness

All available evidence needs to be considered when evaluating a claim – no cherry picking!

Honesty

It is easy to deceive yourself when you want something to be true or when you are emotionally, financially, historically or otherwise invested in a particular claim being true. Evaluate the evidence honestly and face the truth – whatever that might be.

Replication

It should be possible for any evidence in support of a claim to be confirmed in subsequent tests and these tests should have been carried out.

Sufficiency

The amount, type and quality of the evidence in support of a claim should be appropriate to the claim being made. 'The burden of proof is on the claimant.' Claims are not correct until proven incorrect; they are of unknown validity until tested. If you think Elvis is still alive and living on an island somewhere, then lack of refutation is not affirmative proof of this. If you say you can read minds, that claim requires a higher standard of evidence than if you told me you just went to the shops, because the latter is consistent with my current knowledge of what is possible in the world.

7 Getting the information out

This chapter covers the parts of the course that you will be assessed on. Generally speaking, you are assessed on the very skills that are needed in a professional career as a psychologist. That includes conducting research, writing papers, being critical, and so on. The exceptions are your exams – since I don't see psychologists taking exams as part of their job, I can only assume they are part of some sadistic conspiracy to stress out psychology students.

Ultimately, it is not enough to be able to locate, synthesize and criticize psychological theory; you also have to *demonstrate* that you are able to do so in the specific way that they want you to show them. So, you have to play a game: learn what the assessors are looking for and tailor your written work towards it.

In this chapter we will look at:

- essay writing
- lab reports
- your dissertation
- exam strategies

Essay writing

Below is a collection of rules of thumb to help you write excellent essays. I want to make clear that the ideas ahead are guidelines, not fixed rules. You can break any of these 'rules' if you think your essay works better that way.

The very first thing you should do before writing your essay

Step one is to get hold of the marking criteria for the essays. It is not cheating to do this; just ask your lecturer where you can get a copy. These are the guidelines that markers are told to follow when marking work. Usually there is a set of criteria for grades in different areas, such as your use of English, your critical analysis, your understanding of the issues; and you get a mark for each. Your overall grade will be based on these criteria, with more weight given to some (e.g., critical analysis) than others (e.g., referencing).

When you finish the first draft of your essay, go through the criteria for the grade you are aiming to achieve and check your work against it. Of course, there is some subjectivity here in whether your work meets the criteria but it will at least give you an idea of where your work could be improved.

Seven common errors in essay writing

1. Not adhering to the word limit.
2. Essay does not answer the question.
3. Inappropriate evidence used (including personal experience).
4. Answer is not well structured.
5. Written in first person ('I').
6. Does not demonstrate processing.
7. Poor grammar, punctuation or spelling.

This is a little checklist you should go through before handing any essay in to ensure you have not made any of these common mistakes. Make sure you're inside the allotted word limit. Make sure your answer addresses the question and you are not going off on a tangent. Check that your references are all from peer-reviewed journals or books written by well-known researchers – don't back up points with personal experiences or lay articles. Is the answer structured properly? Does it flow logically from point to point or is it a disjointed collection of arguments? Have you written in the first person 'I' at any point (in some essays such as reflective accounts, this is OK – check before submitting). Have you demonstrated your independent thought and analysis or have you simply summarized well-known arguments? Finally, do you need to check your grammar and punctuation?

If you've managed to avoid these pitfalls, you've made great progress towards a good mark.

Choosing an essay question

Sometimes, you will get to choose from a selection of essay questions. How do you choose the best one for you? I recommend weighing up your choice based on the following criteria:

*   interest
*   relevance to your future plans
*   ease
*   crossover into other subject areas.

Interest

The number-one criterion is your personal interest. In my view, there is nothing that would make for a better choice. If a particular topic fascinates you, choose it. Not only will you enjoy the process of studying and writing more but you're more likely to put in the time, stay focused on it and think about the topic more when you're not studying (e.g., you might come up with ideas on the train or in the shower). This is a no-brainer.

Relevance to your future plans

If you are planning to continue in a career that is the same, similar or overlaps with one of the essay topics, this is also a good choice. It will prepare you for the future and give you more knowledge to take into that career, you'll be able to use the fact that you have studied it in detail as a selling point in your job interviews and closer inspection will help you to work out whether you really want to pursue a career in it.

Ease

Some topics just come more easily to you. This could be for any number of reasons: you've studied it or something similar before; you already have some good ideas on it; you know people that know about it and they've talked to you; or maybe you just randomly seem to 'get it'. These topics are obvious good choices in the absence of intrinsic interest in any others.

Crossover into other subject areas

Some topics are very similar to things you've covered in other modules. The two modules might even reference some of the same papers. These crossover topics are good choices because you're getting twice the pay-off for the same amount of work. It's useful to choose a couple of modules that are more 'general'; for example, statistics and evolutionary psychology are two that have some relevance in almost every other module and having a good understanding of them will get you those 'breadth of reading' marks that are so coveted in academic marking schemes.

It's not cheating to adapt material from another topic or module. If you've studied four different modules in a year, this indisputably is breadth of reading – what you get marked on is whether you can show it or not. Just make sure that it's relevant - don't cross over for the sake of it.

Interpretation of essay questions

It's tempting at this point to open up Microsoft Word, write the essay question at the top and get going. But, as you've probably come to expect by now, there is a better way! As I mentioned earlier, one of the common mistakes in essays (and exams) is not answering the question being asked. The most common scenario is when the question says to critically evaluate but the answer gives only a description of the facts. With no evidence of processing, the essay gets a low mark, if it even passes at all. For this reason you need to carefully interpret the essay question.

Your interpretation consists of two phases:

- Phase 1: note the keywords.
- Phase 2: identify the type of question.

Keywords

Here are a few examples. Imagine you're answering this question:

> *Critically evaluate the impact of the relationship between client and therapist on therapeutic effectiveness.*

The keywords here are 'critically evaluate', 'impact', 'relationship' and 'therapeutic effectiveness'.

The first one, 'critically evaluate' tells us the question type. In this case we're evaluating – more on that later. Then we have 'impact'. This tells us we are looking for causality. Our analysis should reflect the strength of cause and effect relationships. Next, 'relationship'. This refers to Carl Rogers' idea that it is the quality of the therapeutic relationship that brings benefits, rather than specific methods or techniques. Finally, 'therapeutic effectiveness'. Positive benefits resulting from psychotherapy.

This guides our answer and our analysis. We're evaluating, so weighing up the strength of the evidence and looking for an 'impact'; a cause–effect relationship. We know that if we find too many correlational studies and too few experiments in the literature, the cause and effect relationship may not be well established. We can use the ideas from our discussion of the scientific method earlier to discover how strong this cause–effect link is. And so on.

Lets try another one:

> *Describe the role of dopamine in the acute effects of cocaine.*

You might get something similar in a drugs and behaviour or neuropsychology class. What are the keywords?

- '*Describe*' is the type of question.
- '*Dopamine*' is a neurotransmitter
- '*Acute effects*' means we're looking at the short-term effects, rather than chronic or long-term effects.
- '*Cocaine*' is a recreational drug.

This question is asking about neurobiological mechanisms. You would explain what cocaine is, what dopamine is, discuss dopamine pathways in the brain and explain how dopamine is involved in the acute effects of the drug. You might include a little bit of evaluation of the evidence but your focus would be on describing the mechanisms.

Table 7.1 The main types of essay question

Evaluation	Compare and contrast	Description
Critically discuss . . .	Compare and contrast . . .	Describe . . .
Critically evaluate . . .	Compare	Explain . . .
To what extent . . .	Contrast	Summarise . . .
Argue . . .	Differentiate . . .	Outline . . .
Discuss	Distinguish . . .	Define . . .

Types of questions

Different essay questions require vastly different types of answers and, if you don't know the differences between question types, it's easy to get caught out. There are three main types, shown in Table 7.1 with some example question phrasing.

These three main types are discussed below individually, along with some basic essay structures you can use. Remember that these guidelines are not set in stone and you should feel free to 'draw outside the lines' and impose your own structure on your essay – particularly where this helps to show your own processing.

Essays

In my opinion, with this type of essay more than any other, you are being assessed on your internal processing. The ability to critically evaluate is the backbone of scientific research, which is why it is so strongly emphasized in your degree. In the first year, you might get to do a few descriptive essays but by the third you will probably be exclusively evaluating.

This type of question wants you to pursue an argument. You need to be critical, which means to point out the strengths and weaknesses of different arguments, positions or theories. This will include a critical discussion of the evidence behind them. At all costs, ensure the bulk of your essay is critical, evaluative and avoids excessive description.

There are two structures you can use in an evaluative essay, which are shown in Table 7.2.

Table 7.2 The two structures you can use in evaluation essays

Structure 1	Structure 2
Introduction	Introduction
All arguments for	Argument for
All arguments against	Argument against
Conclusion	Argument for
	etc. . .
	Conclusion

Introduction

Along with the general guidelines on introductions on page 97, here you might also outline the position you are taking in the essay (e.g., 'This essay will argue that . . .').

Main body

There are two ways to structure the main body. You can discuss all the arguments in support of your position, then the arguments against, or you can alternate discussing arguments for and against throughout (see Table 7.2).

The choice of which structure to use is a tough one and I've pulled many hairs out over this in the past. Unfortunately, there is no single answer to this. But when making your decision, your guiding principle should be the argument itself. Is your argument more or less clear with each of these two structures? Use your plan (page 96) to help you determine this; you might also want to put the main points on index cards or sticky notes and reorder them to give yourself an idea of which one works best in your situation.

Conclusion

Your conclusion should make clear the position of your argument – NOT your opinion on the matter but a preference based on your reasoned discussion of the evidence. The conclusion should express the same position that is consistently pursued through the essay. For example, do not use the whole of the main body arguing for a position and then conclude that it is invalid; keep it congruent. Show that your evaluation of the evidence has determined your position – not the other way around.

How to display originality in evaluation essays

My philosophy on originality is that there are two ways you can display it. You can go after the theory: make some insightful theoretical arguments or criticize the logic of the theory; or you can criticize the method, which would include a discussion of the quality of the studies that support it, including their statistical analyses. It's quite hard to make an original theoretical contribution in an essay but it's quite easy to make an original criticism of the method, because if you work hard on your stats you may well know more than some of the researchers you're writing about! So you can pick up the marks for originality quite easily by criticizing method, rather than theory.

Of course you may have some original theoretical arguments and criticisms to make – particularly if you've taken my advice thus far and spend a lot of time processing and planning. If so, great! But if not, don't worry; the point here is that purely from the perspective of scoring points, you can get those 'originality' marks relatively easily by going after the method.

Reading for a critical analysis

As you are conducting your research for the essay, you will need to read with a critical eye. To do this, I find it is best to make multiple passes of the paper, rather than critique-as-you-go. On the first pass, just read the material as outlined on page 77, selecting and rejecting sections and flagging sections for later scrutiny. When you have done this, then go through the material again with your nitpicking, critical, devil's advocate hat on. If you wish, you could buy some novelty devil horns to wear while you do this (or maybe you already own some).

Compare and contrast questions

A compare and contrast essay will test your ability to analyze two psychological constructs, theories or arguments in terms of their similarities and/or differences. You'll be required to show where these positions share common ground and where they are different. It is less important to evaluate or criticize the evidence, although you would usually include a little evaluation, particularly where it is relevant to the comparison. For example, if theory A and theory B both make a particular claim but the evidence does not apply as strongly to theory B for some reason, criticizing this evidence would be fine, because it might be that they do not share this ground after all.

Note: be perceptive to the question; most of the time you will have to compare and contrast but sometimes you may have to focus on differences or similarities. If you're focusing on differences, mention similarities but don't give them as much space. If you're unsure about how much weight to give to each, check with your lecturers.

Table 7.3 shows the structures you can use for a compare and contrast essay.

Introduction

As well as following the general guidelines for introductions, here is the place to give a brief outline of the two positions you are going to compare. Define your terms and define the

Table 7.3 Possible structures in a compare and contrast essay

Structure 1	*Structure 2*
Introduction	Introduction
All commonalities	Point A – commonalities and differences
All differences	Point B – commonalities and differences
Conclusion	etc. . . .
	Conclusion

positions, then tell the reader that you will compare and contrast these theories. Something along these lines:

- Opening words/define terms.
- Outline theory A.
- Outline theory B.
- 'Although theory A and theory B share many conceptual and empirical similarities, they differ in important ways. This essay will . . .'

This can be over several paragraphs if you wish.

Sometimes you'll be asked to discuss a debate that is currently ongoing in journals. In this case, show you're aware that this is currently a contested area of the research and that you're familiar with the major papers involved in that debate. Your lectures and previous research will have brought the debate to your attention should this be the case.

Main body

Like the evaluation questions, there unfortunately isn't a perfect structure to the main body that will work every time. Your possibilities are shown in Table 7.3.

As you can see, you can either discuss all the commonalities, then all the differences, or you can discuss the positions theme-by-theme. Your choice will depend on your personal preferences and the essay you're doing.

Sometimes it can be useful to bring in a third position in the main body, which you can use to demonstrate commonalities between the theories and show your wider reading. For example, something like 'theory A and theory B both suggest that x. This is in marked contrast to theory C, which states y'. No need to go into detail on theory C; just use it to highlight a commonality and show wider reading.

Conclusion

The conclusion, as always, is quite similar to the introduction. Sum up the comparisons you have made in a new way, talk about the bigger picture and the implications – the usual stuff. See the general guidelines found on page 102 for more details.

Description questions

The description essay is probably the easiest kind to do but, arguably, has the lowest potential to get you a high mark because there is less leeway to demonstrate your processing. It's a fairly simple type of essay; you are making a detailed breakdown of a particular construct, theory or argument, with little space given to things like analysis, evaluation or synthesis of ideas.

Table 7.4 shows how you might structure a description essay.

Table 7.4 Structures you can use in a description essay

Structure 1	Structure 2
Introduction	Introduction
Overview	Overview
Describe detail/aspect A	Detailed breakdown
Supporting evidence/examples	Supporting evidence/examples
Describe detail/aspect B	Evaluation/weaknesses/alternative explanations
Supporting evidence/examples	Conclusion
etc. . . .	
Evaluation/weaknesses/alternative explanations	
Conclusion	

Introduction

The general guidelines on introductions (page 97) will likely be all you need here.

Main body

Once more, we have two possibilities, shown in Table 7.4. Personally, I much prefer the one on the left, because I like to support a statement right after making it. I think it's a good habit to get into – unsupported arguments stick out a mile in academic papers and, since the person marking your paper reads a lot of papers, they will have a keen eye for this sort of thing. However, the structure on the right could work well too in certain circumstances.

Brief evaluation

Like the compare and contrast, it's not necessary to make a detailed evaluation. You might want to point out a few weaknesses of the theory or some competing theories and alternative explanations.

Conclusion

Refer to the general guidelines for conclusions on page 102. Give a quick recap of the key points in your essay and talk about the usefulness of what you have discussed in the real world and as a contribution to the knowledge base. Perhaps mention some other theories and research that it influenced and future directions that might be pursued.

General guidelines on essay writing

The following guidelines apply no matter what question type you are answering.

Doing research for the essay

Once you've completed your interpretation of the question and familiarized yourself with the general structure that the essay might take, it is time to apply what you have learned in the other chapters. Start conducting research for your essay while keeping the question in mind. Look for material that is relevant to the question, take notes, engage with it, develop your understanding and form your own position on it. Once you've done that, you can start making the plan.

Planning and outlining

It's best not to start planning and writing your draft unless you have a good understanding of the topic, have thought about it and could probably dash off a quick draft without referring to books. Try to avoid at all costs the situation where you do a little research, write it up (or like many people, paraphrase a textbook or article), research your next point, then write that up, etc. This is a seriously *stressful* way to write an essay, because you don't know where you're going with it (let alone your poor reader), if indeed you are going anywhere at all! You may end up with something that doesn't flow well, nor display much processing. You'll miss the opportunity to get a bird's-eye view of the topic and how it all links together and your work will end up being very similar to most of the other essays your tutor will read.

Once you understand the topic well, you can start on your plan. It's worth reiterating though, that 'everyone is different' and some people might prefer to write 'on the fly' or write their plan as they go along. I have done some essays this way – start writing the introduction and put bullet points ahead in the document when I think of something. But now I prefer to write a full plan first and believe it's the better way overall.

Why do I think this? Because if you write on the fly, you run a larger risk of missing something important or maybe you remember it later but you've already got beautifully written, flowing paragraphs that you now have to break up to put the new arguments in. To be sure, this sometimes happens when using a full plan; the point is that it's less likely to happen. Also, writing a full plan first allows you to impose your own processing of the material on to the structure of your essay. Otherwise, you might end up copying common structures used in textbooks. Your full plan will reflect your work, your structuring and your processing. In other words, a lot of this 'show your processing' philosophy I'm trying to instil in you will take care of itself simply by using a plan.

Still not convinced? Then I'll also add that it's easier to spot unbalanced and biased arguments by planning beforehand and prevents 'idea floating', where your essay essentially becomes a list of disjointed and unconnected points, floating around rather than being grouped and logically connected.

How to write the essay

Many people have a big fear of essay writing; particularly international students for whom English is not the first language. If you do not have a firm and solid grasp of English grammar and punctuation, this is something you should address immediately. Lynne 1 book, *Eats, Shoots and Leaves,* is probably the only book you will need on punc short, very accessible and very funny. Also check whether your institution classes on English or essay writing – take them if you feel you need them. Yes, go to an extra class but it will pay off later when you produce better work with l

The classic essay writing principle is this:

- Tell them what you're going to tell them.
- Tell them.
- Tell them what you've told them.

That's basically what the introduction, main body and conclusion sections are for, respec- tively. Here are some specific tips for dealing with these different sections of your essays, regardless of what kind of question you're answering.

Introductions

The introduction is similar to an abstract in a journal paper. You're going to tell them what you will tell them. This includes defining your terms and, if necessary, explaining your interpretation of the question. Remember, essays are *academic* pieces of work. You're not trying to be a modern William Shakespeare! Be concise, clear and to the point, rather than wordy, extravagant and poetic – although you can use several paragraphs for your introduction if you need to.

Overall, keep in mind that your introduction is the reader's map for the rest of the essay – don't have them feeling lost!

Five ways to start your essay

The above is the general 'philosophy' around the introduction. Here now are some specific ways to open your essay. Sometimes it's hard to get that first line down on paper and be happy with it, but I hope that one of these will be suitable:

1 START WITH A DEFINITION

Like I said, you're not trying to be a Shakespeare. It's perfectly fine to jump right in with a definition.

> *'Positive psychology is the study of the conditions and processes that contribute to the flourishing or optimal functioning of people, groups and institutions (Gable & Haidt, 2005). In recent years . . .'*

or . . .

'Altruism is defined as behaviour that benefits others at the cost of the lifetime production of offspring by the altruist.'

2 OUTLINE A MAJOR DEBATE

If there are any major debates or issues within the topic in question, here's a good place to demonstrate your awareness of them. Sometimes a question will ask you to compare or discuss an area that is hotly debated. You can explicitly note this:

'Whether serial murder is predominantly caused by biological or environmental factors is an area of contention in the literature. Biological arguments revolve around . . .'

3 PUT THE ISSUE IN CONTEXT

You can outline the wider context in which the evidence you will present has implications:

'The relationship between mind and body has long been of interest to scholars and philosophers. Recently, it has been studied scientifically . . .'

4 START WITH YOUR PURPOSE

Get straight to the point.

'This essay will discuss the role of dopamine in the acute effects of cocaine.'

5 START WITH A QUOTATION

For a great example of starting with a quotation, check out page 5 of this book! I recommend finding something that reflects the tone of your essay. Hence, it is often a good idea to wait until your essay is finished (or at least drafted) before you find a suitable quote.

The main body

The point I want to make above all is that essays are your opportunity to demonstrate the processing you have done with the material. This is your analysis and you should impose your own structure on your essay based on that. Keep in mind that you are being assessed on your cognitive ability to evaluate, compare, analyze, criticize – or whatever – psychological evidence. All of this occurs in a nicely organized main body.

How to make the essay 'flow'

The type of question will determine how the main body will be structured and what kinds of arguments you will include in it. In general though, the main body should flow logically from one paragraph to the next, and your argument should develop throughout the essay. If you do not write it like this, you will end up with a list of unrelated points. Let me show you what paragraphs that do not flow look like.

Always back up a point or argument you make with a reference to a journal paper. Do not leave statements 'hanging' without a reference. You need to give a reason for making the points and arguments that you make and the reader needs to be able to check your sources to see if they agree with you. They should never be in a position where they have to just take your word for it. You can also use multiple citations if you have read several papers that back up a point you make. Just separate them with semi-colons. For example:

> 'Likewise, Japan saw dramatic increases in income during the same period; yet many studies report no discernible increase in well-being. This pattern is typical of a number of nations (Blanchflower & Oswald, 1997; Diener & Oishi, 2000; Biswas-Diener & Diener, 1995).'

So, make the paragraphs flow into each other. In the current paragraph, I've just used a 'recap' sentence to do this. It reminded you what we were talking about, since you might have got a little lost after that big quote. But there are other ways.

One of those ways, as you have now seen, is to end the previous paragraph by hinting at what you will talk about in the next one and then getting straight into it. Remember though, you're writing an academic essay, not a murder mystery, so don't try to build suspense. You're not trying to create an experience for the reader; you are trying to be as clear and concise as possible about what you are saying. To make this easier, 'transition words' can be very useful to move from one paragraph to the next. They make it perfectly and explicitly clear to the reader how the paragraphs link up and what the new one is about, so there's no misunderstanding.

However, transition words are not suitable for every situation. Although they worked well in this paragraph, they can get tiresome with too much use, although if you mix it up a bit you should be OK. There's a box full of useful transition words in Table 7.5.

Table 7.5 Some 'transition words' you can use to link your paragraphs together

Example transition words
However
What is more
Furthermore
Additionally
Firstly/secondly/thirdly/.../finally
In effect
Essentially
Alternatively
On the other hand

So that's how to link paragraphs together. You've been given a few specific ways to do so and I hope you will become a little more conscious of how paragraphs are linked in the papers you read, which will help you see how it's done. Now let's look at what goes on within the paragraph.

The paragraph

As a general rule in academic writing, only cover one topic within a paragraph. Do not make multiple points in one paragraph unless they are part of the same general argument and there is a good reason they should be together. Whether you cover one point or more, the paragraph will typically start with a statement declaring what the paragraph is about. This is often called the 'topic sentence' and, if you look over the previous section, you will see that each paragraph had a clear topic sentence.

Some people are also concerned about paragraph length. There is no rule that says all paragraphs have to be a certain length. In fact, I think it's better to vary the length of paragraphs. If you are using headers, it can also be useful to use a very short paragraph before each new header, to act as a signpost to the new topic you're moving into.

If you're not permitted to use headings in your essay, or if you don't want to, you might use a 'recap paragraph', which will do much the same job. Simply summarize what you have just been talking about and introduce the next topic. This can be particularly effective if your next section addresses a limitation in the evidence just presented. For example:

> 'Although the evidence thus presented is robust and well-replicated, the correlational nature of the studies prevents cause-effect interpretations. To make such inferences requires data from experimental research, of which there are three primary studies. The first . . .'

Generally speaking, after you have delivered your topic sentence, you should use the rest of the paragraph to expand on this and to cite any evidence that you need to back up the points you have made.

The sentence

I don't want to go into grammar, sentence structure and things like that. As I said earlier, get *Eats, Shoots and Leaves* by Lynne Truss or seek extra instruction if you need help with that. I just want to make one important point: keep your sentences short and concise where possible.

If you write long-winded sentences you will end up losing your reader because they won't have that opportunity to mentally stop for a second and get their bearings and, also, long sentences are rare in the material we read so when we do come across them they seem odd, although sometimes long sentences do work better than lots of shorter ones (not this time, though!). But don't fall into the opposite trap. Short sentences get annoying too. They work against the flow. Especially when too frequent. Wait, was that a Haiku?

Voice and style

Psychological papers, you may have noticed, are a little dry and emotionless. You don't get papers that say:

> *'A deep silence filled the room as we began to analyze the data. The smell of anticipation filled our senses; the air was thick with tension. Nothing could have prepared me for what was about to happen. Wiping the sweat from my brow, I signalled the analyst to begin.'*

For one thing, research isn't that exciting, but the main reason is that putting emotional language into a paper might influence the reader's interpretation of it. We don't want that: we want them to be unbiased, to look at the data and make their own decision on it. For this reason, avoid emotive language. Don't say that results were incredible. Say they were highly unexpected or counterintuitive, or something like that. Keep the language dry and scientific.

Speaking of which, you'll also have noticed that scientific papers use highly technical language. In my view, this sometimes goes beyond practicality and I wonder whether some researchers are using complex language just for the sake of it. Don't make the same mistake. Remember your goal – a clear and concise demonstration of your processing – and your knowledge of the topic. Don't use complex words for the sake of complexity. If a 'big' word fits with the flow of your sentence and makes sense, use it; but never use a word you don't fully understand just because you think it looks scientific. You should appear confident in your use of English (and psychological terminology) but you will not appear so if you use a word incorrectly.

The best way to develop a scientific writing voice is to practise often and get feedback on your work but I have another tip for developing the academic writing style. I've written for several blogs over the years and it helped me to notice that what I have been recently reading strongly influences my writing style. If I spend a few days toiling over a few technical journal papers for an assignment, my blogs get more formal, more academic. If I've spent a day reading Bill Bryson, they get a little jovial and I throw a few jokes in.

This is the power of reading on writing. Whatever you read a lot of, you find your writing moving slightly towards. Reasoning forward, if you read a lot of academic papers, your essay writing will become more academic. Popular books written for the lay audience will not typically bestow upon you a suitable writing style, although there are some exceptions (e.g., Richard Dawkins). For this reason, as well as for your general studies, try to spend some time every day reading journal articles. Even if you just spend 15 minutes reading a couple of pages, it will keep the academic writing style fresh in your mind and, even if it doesn't, you're making constant progress on your reading.

Recap main points

Recap by giving a shortened, synthesized and condensed version of your main argument. Do not give your opinion (unless specifically asked by the essay question) but explain what the evidence points towards on balance. What you say in the conclusion should reflect the balance of the main body and the strength of the arguments you have presented. As I said earlier, don't evenly balance the main body and have the conclusion strongly leaning to one side – such a conclusion would not be justified by your arguments.

Future directions

It's customary in science to end papers with suggestions for future research. You could note any gaps in the evidence and arguments and suggest areas for future inquiry; particularly where you have highlighted areas as being weakly supported in your main body.

The conclusion

Once you get to the conclusion, it's normal to feel a great sense of relief that you're almost finished! Now you need to 'tell them what you've told them' and perhaps discuss the implications and future directions of the topic in question. Do not present any further arguments or evidence in the conclusion.

Here are some specific suggestions – you may use some or all of these, depending on what you think best for your particular paper.

Wider implications

You can also add in what the wider implications of the research are in the real world. Check your marking criteria, as you may be being marked on your ability to see the 'big picture' and how the theory might be applied.

Repeat the question

One good way to start the conclusion is to restate the essay question. This is particularly effective if you are able to use headings in your essays (sometimes you are not – check with the person who marks your work). The heading could be 'Conclusion and future directions' and the first sentence, the question being asked (not verbatim, just the gist of it):

> *'Conclusion and future directions*
> *Does the relationship between client and counsellor have an impact on therapeutic outcomes? The evidence is . . .'*

Be thought provoking

If there is one thing to keep in mind with your conclusion, it is to be thought provoking. If your conclusion – especially your very last sentence – is thought provoking, you will leave your reader feeling impressed and clever. If this is not possible, then the principles of clarity and concision will not steer you wrong.

Editing and revising

There will always be ways to improve your first draft. Maybe there are grammatical errors, factual errors, maybe something can be worded more clearly. I have gone through this book numerous times, yet you still might find a few mistakes. We're only human, you and I (with apologies to any artificial or extra-terrestrial intelligence that may someday read this).

That's why the editing and revising process is so important. No one gets it right first time. It can really help to read your essay out loud. Sentences that are perfectly clear when you're whizzing through might seem clumsy when read out. Remember, you have been staring at your work for a long time; you're probably blind to some errors you have made.

Another useful thing to do is to get someone else to read it. Use the principle of reciprocity. Buy them a small gift like a cup of coffee and ask if they wouldn't mind reading it because it would really help you out. This is a particularly useful thing to do if English is not your first language. Obviously, if you are given the option to get an essay draft looked at by a lecturer or other relevant person, grasp it with both hands (the opportunity, that is, not the lecturer).

Of course, there's always the little matter of the word count. More often than not, you'll miss the word count. Either you've overshot the mark (most commonly) and need to trim the work down or you've undershot and you need to expand and add new points. The best position to be in is to have written too much and then have to cut back a little.

The reason for this is that first drafts are often quite 'flabby'. There are usually many places in which you can be more economical with your words and, simply by focusing on concision, you might end up bringing your essay back within the word limit, without sacrificing any of your arguments.

However, this is not always the case and sometimes you will get to the point where you must remove whole sections of your work. This is difficult. It's hard to give up sections you've worked hard on and put processing time into. But you'll have to discover your ruthless streak if you're over the word limit. The deciding factor should always be the relevance of the material to the question. If you can't decide between parts to remove, don't just guess; do some tests. Which do you think you can remove but leave your argument the most convincing? Make a back up copy, then do some cutting and pasting of different parts. Read through, and try again with another section. Which version was better?

You should also check your reasoning. If you've followed the advice in the book so far, you should be getting fairly familiar with critical analysis, so apply the same critical eye that you would use on journal papers to your own work. Are there gaps in your argument? Is it unbalanced or biased? Have you made any unsupported assumptions? Are your arguments too strong based on the evidence you present? It's always a good idea to check these things.

Referencing

Here's a piece of advice that can save you hours of work in the future – collect all your references as you go along! Don't wait until you've completed the essay, then go back and find all the papers you have cited. This will take a long time, cause a lot of hassle and there will always be that one pesky paper you can't find. It's also a good idea to save a copy of every paper you read to your hard drive, for easy access.

When referencing, keep your citations on a separate document and keep it open when you are working on your essay. When you cite a paper, immediately put the reference in the document, properly formatted in American Psychological Association (APA) style. If you prefer, you can get a program like endnote.com or similar to do it for you but, if you are writing references manually, a good tip is to Google the paper as it would be referenced in-text, with quotations around it. For example, by Googling 'Bowlby (1969)' I'll be presented with a list of websites who have the full citation in their reference list, very often in APA format, and I can just copy and paste.

If you're stuck on the correct formatting for APA references, don't worry! I know it seems confusing and petty at first and, yes, all the punctuation and spacing has to meet the exact APA rules. Don't worry though, with time and practice it becomes second nature. There are some great videos explaining this at: flash1r.apa.org/apastyle/basics/index.htm. There are also quick-reference guides for the more common types of references in Appendix C.

Avoiding plagiarism

Your tutors will have drilled this in to you, so I will only mention it briefly. Plagiarism is never a good idea. For one thing, it's cheating. You're passing off someone else's work as your own. For another, you will not develop a strong grasp of the material if you just repeat what someone else has said.

Some people will paraphrase work that exists. They'll find a textbook chapter or journal paper on the topic and rewrite it so that it is unrecognizable. This often happens when people start their essay the day before it is to be handed in! Again, it's a bad idea. You won't get a high mark because the essay will display no originality and little evidence of processing or wide research. The lecturers know the subject well and they know the main papers that often get cited. While you are not technically committing plagiarism in this case, it's just not a good strategy.

What is more, it's not good for you, either. Anyone can paraphrase a textbook. You're not challenging your brain, you won't retain anything you write and you'll get a low mark. Why someone would want to waste their limited time on this earth copying textbooks, is beyond me. If you are consistently compelled to do so, consider whether this is really the course for you.

Lab reports

Most of the advice on essay writing applies to lab reports too. Things like concision, style and flow apply to all written assignments. However, lab reports are structured a little differently, according to the rules of the APA. There is a useful series of videos by the APA at: flash1r.apa.org/apastyle/basics/index.htm.

A lab report communicates a piece of research to the reader in a very specific and systematic way. You'll do a lot of these throughout your degree. It consists of the following sections:

- title
- abstract
- introduction
- method.

Title

A title should be attention grabbing and accurate. You have a little leeway to add in some humour and creativity if you like (though gauge this on the personality of the person who will be marking the report):

> *'The tooth, the whole tooth and nothing but the tooth: how belief in the Tooth Fairy can engender false memories' (Principle & Smith, 2007)*

Sometimes researchers link in a common term or phrase:

> *'On putting the horse before the cart: Exploring conceptual bases of word order via acquisition of a miniature artificial language' (Byrne & Davidson, 1985)*

You don't have to use a common phase either. Something that captures the essential meaning of the findings will work fine too:

> *'It's too difficult! Frustration intolerance beliefs and procrastination' (Harrington, 2005)*

Of course, you can never go wrong with an accurate and concise description:

> *'Short sleep duration is associated with poor performance on IQ measures in healthy school-age children' (Gruber et al., 2010)*

Whatever you do, don't be vague. 'On putting the horse before the cart' alone might be a good title for a magazine article – it's catchy, and has a nice sense of mystery about it – but it's not specific enough for a journal. The accurate description has to be present in addition to the clever bit.

Abstract

An abstract gives the reader the most important information contained within the report in around 250 words. Don't copy and paste from the paper itself but write it separately and always after the full report is completed. Describe the question that the research is asking, why it's being asked, how the study was conducted and what the results and conclusions were. If you wish, you can use a structure:

Background:
Objectives:
Methods:
Results:
Conclusions:

Introduction

The aim of the introduction is to provide a rational for your study. Generally speaking, the structure of the introduction should be like an inverted triangle, starting with the general and moving to the specific. See Figure 7.1 for a diagram of what I mean.

Method

The method section should allow anyone reading the paper to be able to repeat the test on their own, should they want to. The method section is itself broken down into subsections:

- participants
- materials
- design
- procedure
- results
- discussion.

Participants

Who were the participants in the experiment? How many were there? How were they recruited? Give a breakdown of their demographic details if you have collected these data – ages (mean and standard deviation), ethnicity (as percentages and actual figures) and gender (percentages and actual figures). Also give details on the number of dropouts and whether any participants were removed from the analysis for any reason.

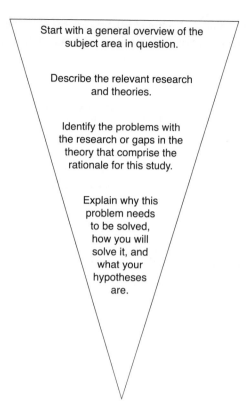

Start with a general overview of the subject area in question.

Describe the relevant research and theories.

Identify the problems with the research or gaps in the theory that comprise the rationale for this study.

Explain why this problem needs to be solved, how you will solve it, and what your hypotheses are.

Figure 7.1 How to write an introduction to a lab report

Materials

Describe the materials, instruments, equipment and stimuli that were used in the experiment. If you are using self-report (questionnaire) measures, give the psychometric properties of each scale, including test–retest correlations and internal consistency alphas. You can find this information from any other study that has used that measure, along with the relevant references.

Design

Describe the design of the experiment, what the independent variables were and the levels of each IV. Was the design correlational? Between subjects? Was it a 2×2 design?

Procedure

The procedure is a step-by-step description of what you did. When were the questionnaires and instructions given, how, and by whom? What did the participants do, where did they do it and how did they do it? Was it in a lab or a natural setting? When were results collected and how? Were there any specific procedures that you had to follow? When and how were participants debriefed?

Results

In the results section you tell the reader what you found. Describe the statistical analyses used. You might use tables and graphs if you feel that it helps to get the information across. You'll want to give the means and the standard deviations of the results for each of your groups or variables, as well as the results of the analyses. Also, describe the results in words. Don't include any interpretation of discussion of the results, just present the data.

Discussion

The discussion section should generally take the shape of a triangle, opposite to the direction of the introduction: moving from specific discussion of your study to the wider implications of the results on the theory. See Figure 7.2 for a diagram of this.

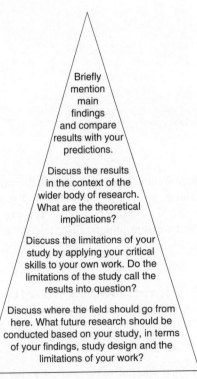

Figure 7.2 How to write the conclusion of a lab report

Your dissertation

Your dissertation might well be the single biggest piece of work you've ever done. It can be incredibly fulfilling to complete such a mammoth task, but I'm not going to lie – it can also be immeasurably frustrating. In terms of the write-up, the sections on essay writing and lab reports should serve you well enough, so here I'll just cover choosing a topic and actually conducting the research.

Choosing a topic

Contrary to popular belief, finding a topic that's likely to get you a high mark in a field you're interested in actually takes very little effort. Simply follow these steps.

1. Choose a subject area.
2. Find a suitable topic.
3. Identify your dissertation question.
4. Check out your supervisor's idea.

Choose a subject area

First, decide on the broad subject area you want to spend some time looking into. By the time you get to your dissertation, you'll have been exposed to a large number of sub-fields within psychology and you'll have a good idea of which you like and which you don't. The number one ultimate deciding factor above all else should be your interest in the topic. If there's a sub-field or class that you enjoyed more than the others, pick that one. If any of them get you excited, or if you think about them a lot, these are good choices too. Beyond that, the criteria on page 88 should help, with one addition: The *supervisor*.

You'll have to find a supervisor for your project, who you report to and discuss your progress with. If there is really no particular subject area that stands out to you, think about who might make a good supervisor in terms of how much you like them, how much rapport you have with them, how much support you are likely to get and their availability. If there's a specific supervisor you really want, I recommend you show your enthusiasm by completing many of the following steps and showing them your ideas so far. If you appear to be hard-working and passionate about the topic, you've got a much better chance.

Find a suitable topic

When you know the broad subject area you want to do your work in, the same ultimate overriding factor applies to finding a more specific topic within that area: personal interest. If you've chosen cognitive psychology as your subject area, which area within cognitive psychology do you like the most? Don't choose language if you find memory fascinating: follow your interests. Again, use the criteria on page 88 if nothing stands out.

Identify your dissertation question

After choosing a more specific topic area, you'll need to come up with a specific research question you want to ask. Again, there is a very simple rule of thumb that makes this very easy – aim to make an original contribution to the field. Don't be intimidated: paradoxically, this is actually the easiest way to go about your dissertation.

Think back to the scientific cycle we discussed at the start of this book. Your job is to enter that cycle with your own piece of research. Some people on your course will pick topics that are, to varying degrees, a little more 'random' than others. Maybe they choose topics that are interesting to them personally but aren't a contribution to the field because they don't enter the cycle to add to or question what is already known.

How do we know how to enter the cycle? Exactly the same way the people who do this for a living do it. The first step is to read a number of recent papers in your chosen topic area. If you're interested in this area, you're probably familiar with many of them already. If you read five to six of the most recent papers on a topic, you'll have a very good idea of where the frontier of that field is, and what specific studies need to be conducted to move it forward. Why? Because researchers state these things explicitly in the discussion sections of the papers! All you have to do is highlight a potential study that is feasible for you to do, and get started.

By choosing a topic this way, a huge amount of the hard work is done for you by default. Your rationale will be clear and the relevant background research to your study will be well known to you from introduction sections of the papers you've already read. It will be a simple task to write your introduction based on this. The design of your study may also be obvious – particularly if it's a replication, in which case all the work is done. Your discussion section will be easier to write, because you have already identified what the theoretical implications of the results will be by reading the future directions sections of current papers in the area.

Let's walk through an example. Kashdan and Breen (2007) conducted a correlational study, finding that materialism – the occupation with money and material possessions – has an inverse relationship with wellbeing. In other words, materialistic people tend to be less happy. But their study is cross-sectional. In their comments on future directions, they note that experimental studies are needed to see whether materialism actually causes diminished wellbeing. There's an ideal dissertation topic!

The introduction pretty much writes itself by following up the studies that Kashdan and Breen have referenced in their introduction, plus a little extra reading.

The design of the study is decided already – experimental. The measurement tools to use are decided also (the same as Kashdan and Breen or a similar study used, for ease of comparison). A little thought is needed on how to experimentally alter materialism; but, other than that, the hard work is done. It's important to note here that experimental studies, or studies with more than one time-point, will be more of a headache to conduct. Cross-sectional studies analyzed with regression and correlation will be the easiest for you to do – but arguably the least impressive, too.

The implications of the study are clear, too – perhaps materialism causes diminished wellbeing – or maybe diminished wellbeing causes materialism. Are people seeking material possessions as a way of dealing with their low wellbeing or does our materialistic society make people less happy? The answer to this question has wide implications! An experimental design will help to pry these possibilities apart. So the discussion section is fairly easy to write.

That's an example of how to find a dissertation topic with the potential to achieve a high mark and which will help you to learn more about the field. You might even end up with something worth publishing in a journal. By the way, you might have guessed this, but the above is a real life example – it's the specific process I went through when designing and conducting my master's dissertation project. Don't say I don't practise what I preach! Feel free to do the exact same project if you need an idea and this sounds interesting to you.

Your supervisor's idea

Your supervisor (or potential supervisor) will have some good ideas for studies. Another way to come up with a great project idea is to get them to tell you one! However, you should not simply approach them and expect them to do all the work. This sends all the wrong signals. Come up with a few ideas of your own, and take them to your ideal supervisor. Then ask them if they have any suggestions. If you like their idea better than your own, then do it.

Collecting your data

The number one rule of dissertations is start early. Actually, that's also the number two rule. Do not underestimate how much time your dissertation will take. Between data collection, analysis and write up, you potentially have several months of solid work if you want to do a good job. Give yourself plenty of time. The way to do this is to start collecting data as soon as you can, which means not procrastinating on choosing a topic and finding a suitable supervisor.

Planning the study design

Below are ten questions and answering these should result in a guide to completing your dissertation. As always, this should not be seen as set in stone or 100 per cent comprehensive, and the various tasks you'll need to complete will vary depending on your particular project. At this point, I'm assuming that you have chosen a subject area, a topic within that subject area and have a specific idea of what you want to investigate.

1) What research design is most appropriate to your research question?

Are you looking for a cause–effect relationship? Does your question require an experimental design? Is it exploratory? Are you looking for a relationship between variables? Will you be using qualitative or quantitative methodology?

2) How many groups will you have?

Will you need a control group? How many experimental conditions do you need? Bear in mind that the more groups you have, the more participants you need, and the longer it will take to collect your data. However, the more impressive will be the result.

3) What is/are the IV/s? What is/are the DV/s?

What is your independent variable? What are you manipulating? If you are using multiple regression, what are your predictor variables? What is the dependant variable? What are you measuring?

4) How will you measure the DV?

An important question. What scales, instruments or equipment will you use to measure the DV? Will you use self-report scales? What are the advantages and disadvantages of doing so? If you need your study to relate to previous research, it may be prudent to use the same instruments for easier comparison.

   If you are using multiple scales to measure a DV, or if you have multiple DVs, what order will you give the questionnaires in?

5) When will you collect data?

At what time-points do you measure the DV? If you're using a cross-sectional design, this is easy – once. If it's a before-and-after design, will it be for one hour, one day, one week or more?

6) Who are your participants?

Do you need a particular demographic for your study (e.g., gender, ethnic group, socioeconomic status, etc.)? Does your sample need to be representative of a wider population? If so, which population, and how will you prevent any bias in your recruitment? This leads us to . . .

7) How many participants will you need?

As a minimum, I recommend you try to recruit 30 participants for each level of the IV or for each variable in a regression. The more data you can collect, the more chance you have of detecting an effect, should there be one there to detect.

8) How will you recruit participants?

How are you physically going to do this? Will you solicit people face-to-face, ask your friends and family, people on the street? Or will you use the internet? If you can use the internet, I recommend that you do so, because it allows for greater automation of a lot of processes. For example, you can put your surveys online with a service like surveymonkey. com, which will collate your results into a spreadsheet for you to download. You can then use a formula in Microsoft Excel to score the questionnaires. You will have no need to bother with collecting paperwork and typing up the results. As long as your formulae are correct, you have just saved yourself hours of work and taken human error out of the equation; however, you'll probably have to pay for the privilege, unless you can get a similar service via your university. A note of caution, however – be sure to check and double-check all your online surveys for errors and make several 'dummy' runs to ensure that everything works as intended.

As for actual recruitment, you can list your survey on sites like craigslist.org, gumtree.com, as well as more specific sites and discussion forums related to your topic area. Do a Google search and try to find as many blogs on your chosen topic area. Then email the authors and ask if they wouldn't mind mentioning your study to their readers. In this case, it might be best to set up a little website that gives details of your study and how to participate, as this looks professional and makes it easy for bloggers to promote your study. You can set up a free blog at wordpress.com or blogger.com, which will suffice for this purpose.

There are also online services through which you can pay for research participants. Local market research companies may be able to help too. This may not necessarily be for you, and they are probably better suited to cross-sectional designs and regression based studies, as such services are typically set up for market research, which mostly involves collecting data at only one time-point rather than controlled experimental research. However, if you need a lot of data or if you need to collect them in a hurry, this might be an option for you – if you have the cash!

9) How will you randomize?

If you are randomizing group assignment, I recommend that you use random.org. Alternatively, if your questionnaires are online, you can use something called a 'redirect script' to direct people randomly to one of the different web pages your questionnaires are hosted on. Explaining how to do this is beyond the scope of this book; the process is a little complicated. There is a free redirect script at spyka.net/scripts/red/random-redirection-script and if you can upload this to a website you'll be able to use it. Seek assistance from someone who is technically minded if this is making little sense to you.

10) How will you analyze the data?

You should know the answer to this question long before you collect any data. Depending on your study, more exotic analyses may be required that I haven't covered in this book. Maybe you'll do a factor analysis or an ANCOVA. Whatever analysis you do, study it intensely. Make yourself an expert on it. Not only will this help you understand your own results in greater depth but your results section will also be far more polished because you will be more comfortable with and confident about what you are reporting.

These ten questions will give you a decent study design and good understanding of what will be involved in completing your research. Certainly, it will be enough to take with you when you see your supervisor and, from there, you can discuss the finer points together. You should also read the section on goal setting on page 121, which will help you set intermittent deadlines for the various steps you'll have to complete as you progress towards your final paper.

Exam strategies

Personally, I'm not a fan of exams as an assessment technique. The only time you experience exam conditions is in an exam. I find it illogical to be assessed in a situation that you won't ever be in again. Yes, I understand that they challenge certain relevant abilities: time management, dealing with pressure, memory, and so on. I get that. But if I want to assess your potential to be an Olympic sprinter, I don't watch you do the high jump, even though that assesses certain relevant abilities: speed, leg strength, timing, etc. I'd rather just watch you sprint.

Besides, I don't remember all that much from my exams, even the ones I passed with high marks. Why? Because I don't need to. If I ever need that information again I know I can look it up. Interestingly, I remember more from the topics I wrote papers on than those I took exams for.

Anyway, enough complaining! Exams exist, so we just have to play the game until they don't. Luckily, they are not an insurmountable obstacle. Far from it. Doing well in exams is a matter of three things:

1. Having a deep understanding of the topic.
2. Preparing well.
3. Dealing with stress.

We've covered point 1 in the previous chapters – having a study schedule, reading, questioning, reflecting. In this section we'll look at points 2 and 3.

Preparing for exams

Ideally, you should not be learning new things within two weeks of the exam. The weeks leading up to the exam should be spent *preparing* for the exam; reviewing material, doing recall tests, plugging gaps in your knowledge, mind mapping your understanding, doing practice exams, and so on. NOT starting a topic for the first time!

Looking up the past exam papers for each subject can be an enlightening exercise. You can get an idea of the wording and style of the questions and you can sometimes get an idea of the exact question that will be asked. This is called 'question spotting' and your lecturers will tell you not to do this. This is partly to cover their asses but also because people who rely on question spotting are not learning the subject, they are just trying to pass an exam on it. This is not the point of going to university to study a subject and it's not the way to get a good grade either.

That said, I recommend that you *do* question spot – but, and I stress, *do not rely on it under any circumstances!* I once took an exam on the biological basis of psychological disorders. About 90 per cent of the lecture slides were on schizophrenia. The exam question for the previous five years or so was on schizophrenia. This is before I started taking my studies more seriously, so naturally I hadn't done any work. At all. As a last resort I made the decision to question spot. I spent one night preparing an answer on schizophrenia that I thought would at least get me a pass. It turned out to be a bad move: the exam was on depression. I tried to think back but couldn't remember a single thing and had to walk out of the exam room after ten minutes. In front of everybody. They all knew what I had done. Pretty embarrassing.

Look, I understand that there will be a certain percentage of people reading this a couple of weeks or less away from an exam they are not prepared for, looking for some way out of this mess. To you, I would offer the following information. Here in the UK, if you fail an exam, the re-sit is always capped at the minimum mark (40 per cent); no matter how spectacular it is. If you question spot and fail, you're destined for 40 per cent, no matter what. If you can cover each topic to the point where you could give a 40 per cent answer (which is not that hard; in one exam I got eight per cent for just a plan!), then you're in a better position to justify question spotting, because that way you might get a half-decent mark but, even if your question doesn't come up, you'll at least get roughly 40 per cent and not have the hassle of a re-sit (which can really ruin a summer, trust me). On the other hand, you could keep covering all potential topics as much as you can and try to push that minimum 40 per cent up a little higher.

So what do you do? It all depends on the number of exams you have left in the course overall, how much weight each one contributes to your final grade and how many of your exams overall contribute to your final grade. For example, if you do ten exams in your course but only the top eight go towards your final mark, you might be best off gambling on question spotting (after covering your 40 per cent minimum of course). Remember the golden rule: *do not rely on question spotting under any circumstances.*

Practice exams

If you have spotted a few questions that might come up or you just want to test your knowledge in a particular area, do a few practice exams. I liked to set a timer for 1 hour and try to answer the question under exam conditions but this can be quite time-consuming and draining (although it does strengthen your hand so you don't get cramps during the real thing!).

If you prefer, you can just practise making plans for the questions. Draw plans however you prefer – I preferred to draw my plans in mind map form (easier to remember) but you can use bullets, lists, whatever you like. Check your practice plans against your notes and fill in anything you missed. You now have a full plan for that topic. Your next task is to ensure that you can write it up when the exam comes. That means recall tests and using the memory techniques described earlier (page 63).

If you have a good knowledge of the subject, plus a few plans memorized that you can recall at will, I guarantee that people will comment on how relaxed you look on the day of the exam!

If you have the time and inclination, however, I strongly recommend going beyond plans and doing a few practice exams; you might come up with some interesting ideas and ways of explaining things that you can develop and build on. Plus, you get an idea of how long it takes you to write about a certain topic and you get better at turning plans into essays. The more practice you get, the better. Some of my exams I had practised so much that I was actually getting bored with writing about those topics. Needless to say, I got the highest marks while experiencing the lowest stress for these subjects.

On the day of the exam

A little physical activity can boost cognitive performance for a while afterwards, in the form of more focus, cognitive flexibility and more retention of information. If you don't believe me, try doing moderate exercise before one of your practice exams or recall tests and you'll see what I mean – it works. So if you saw a tall, handsome but unshaven man running towards the University of East London at around exam time in 2008, it wasn't because I was late for my exam; I was simply attempting to boost my cognitive faculties! And that is the story I'm sticking with.

So, assuming you don't have a condition that makes light exercise dangerous for you, get your blood pumping before the exam. Walk briskly to the exam room, run up and down some stairs – anything you can do to get moving will help. Don't tire yourself out though. Either keep it moderate for 20–40 minutes or, if you prefer higher-intensity exercise, keep it short – two sets of three minutes with a two minute break in-between.

Also, make sure you eat well. Don't overeat of course but make sure you have a meal containing complex carbohydrates (flapjacks worked well for me). If you only eat a chocolate bar before you go in, your body will release insulin to compensate for the increase in blood sugar and you will get hungry again quickly. No one likes a rumbling stomach in the exam room, plus your mental performance will suffer if you're hungry.

Be careful not to go to the opposite extreme either. Although adding protein or fat to a meal can help slow digestion, chowing down on three burgers isn't a good idea – your body will be spending resources on digestion that you would prefer to be sent to the brain!

In the exam room

OK, you're fuelled, you've done some *light* physical activity, you're inside the exam hall and sat down. Now what?

1. *Try to relax*. You will see scores of people furiously reading notes. Some people do not recommend this but I found it very useful to keep a mind map or a few plans in my pocket to go over before going in. More than putting the information into my head, ready to pour out, I found it useful in getting my mind in the right gear for the task ahead.

2. *Write out your plans for each question before writing the actual answers to any of them*. Your stress level is only going to increase as the time limit runs down, so the start of the exam is the best time for recall – do it all at once. A second very important reason to do your plans first is that you'll then have a better idea of which questions will be the easiest. Your recall might be incredible for one question but so-so for another. Always do the easiest question first! Easy questions take a finite amount of time to finish; get them out of the way so you know how much time you have left for the other questions.

3. *Set yourself a time limit for each exam question*. When you reach the end of that time, move on to the next question, and come back to it if you have time later. Make sure you allow yourself enough time to plan at the beginning and to check your answer at the end.

4. *Take in some water and a snack or energy drink*. Spending a few hours without food doing mentally challenging activities uses up glucose. You will get hungry and, if there is less glucose to send to your brain, your performance will suffer slightly. Take something with you as a precaution against this.

Writing the answer

Look at the question very carefully. Just as with essays, there are different types of question that you will be required to answer. Put a box around the instruction words – compare and contrast, describe, critically evaluate, etc. Refer to page 91 for descriptions on how to answer each of these questions. Underline the other keywords in the question. Above all, ensure you are answering the question that is being asked of you! Do not go off on a tangent if it is not relevant to the question. You need to demonstrate that you can pull relevant knowledge from your brain and shape it into the answer to the question being asked.

Many people make mistakes in exams through writing long, complex answers to questions that have not been asked. Perhaps they describe when they are asked to evaluate or they get a technical term confused with something else. Read the instructions carefully; check, double check and triple check. It's useful to be a little neurotic at this stage.

Remember: examiners are not looking for a masterpiece in an exam; you do not have to demonstrate your flair with the written word. It's a science exam, so get to the point quickly and concisely. Do not be vague or general. Give plenty of empirical supporting evidence for your points (just the author name and year is sufficient, the full reference is not needed). Make sure you refer to the course material and recommended reading as well as demonstrating your further reading and reflection. Include your criticisms of the studies when relevant.

Multiple choice exams

If you have a multiple choice exam, rejoice! They are far easier than essay questions. The questions themselves contain a number of memory cues, so you're not recalling from nothing. Plus you have a much better idea of how well you have done before you even leave the exam room. Here's how to approach them:

1. As with essay exams, go through and answer the easy questions first. Make a first pass and answer the questions you definitely know. At this point, you may have already passed!
2. Make a second pass. Look at the questions you are not sure about and see if you can definitely eliminate some of the answers. Usually, there are two options that are obviously incorrect and two more that are very similar and hard to choose between. If you can eliminate the two definitely wrong options, you have a 50–50 chance on each of these questions. Don't actually answer them yet, just cross off the definitely not-correct options.
3. Look at the questions remaining, then identify the ones you definitely cannot answer. By this I mean you literally, truly have no clue whatsoever. Then just take a guess on these questions.
4. Go back to the questions you are not sure about. Now you can devote all your time to these without worrying about the others. Try to trigger your memory. Think back to your flashcards and recall tests, your mind maps, the papers you have read, the discussion you have had, the lectures you went to. Look carefully at the question. Read the options slowly in your mind a few times, one by one. Sometimes it will come back to you in a flash. Other times, it will come back to you in a flash two minutes after you've left the exam room! Try not to strive for the answer, just relax, take a deep breath and let it come to you. If you still don't know, you'll have to guess. You don't lose points for incorrect answers (at least, I've never heard of this – certainly check with your lecturers), so make sure you answer all the questions.

Coping with pre-examination stress

The best way to deal with examination stress is to prepare properly. I hope you have been given enough tips and tools to prepare pretty well. But even if you do, there will always be some stress on the day. You're being assessed on your abilities. It matters. So you feel stress. Here are just a few tips to help you manage the stress on the day:

Minimal caffeine: do not drink too much caffeine on the day. This will only activate you. If you are tired it can give you a welcome boost and improve your concentration. Some people reach for the coffee as a way of coping with the negative feelings of stress. If you drink too much though, you'll be jittery. Having said that, if you're a regular coffee drinker then don't abstain from caffeine on the day, as this can cause a headache – probably the last thing you want.

Relax: take some deliberate steps to relax on the day. Try some relaxing music, relaxation exercises or meditation. Spend some time in a natural environment or green space if you can.

Exercise: as well as improving physical health and cognitive function, moderate exercise can also give your mood a boost too. Is there anything it can't do? Take it easy and stick to within approximately 60–80 per cent of your target heart rate (roughly 220 beats/minute minus your age). Now is not the time to go for a personal best in your powerlifting routine! So 20 minutes of brisk walking just before the exam might help with stress levels. To cover my ass, I should probably advise you to see a doctor before doing any exercise.

Focus on things that are in your control: at this point, what's done is done; there will be little you can actually do to further prepare. Focus on what you can control, not on what you can't. You can control yourself on the day, your travel arrangements and the food you will eat. You can go over the ideas in your head or do some recall tests. You can't control what questions will come up, and you can't go back in time and do more study. So don't focus on these things.

8   Organization and productivity

As a field, psychology has made massive contributions to productivity. Psychologists know a great deal about what motivates people, how goal setting affects performance, how to replenish mental fatigue and many more interesting things. But, for some reason, this isn't trickling down to students to help them study – or at least, not as well as I would like. You can master the most effective study skills ever devised but if you start your essay three days before the deadline and can't resist a quick look on Facebook every ten minutes, it's not going to do you any good. This section is about organizing yourself so that you'll get more done in less time. As a bonus, this will also reduce your stress levels at exam time. There are five steps:

1.   Goal setting.
2.   Organization.
3.   Planning.
4.   Improving motivation and reducing procrastination.
5.   Improving performance on the task at hand.

Step 1 – Goal setting

Everyone sets and pursues goals. Some people are more systematic about it than others but we all set goals implicitly. When you started the course, was it not for a particular goal? To get a certain grade? To move toward a chosen career? To avoid the real world? Goal pursuit is one of the most well researched areas in psychology and the research consistently shows that people who consciously set goals perform better than those who don't. Goals help us to regulate our physical and cognitive effort, they direct our attention to stimuli relevant to our goal, filter our irrelevant stimuli and give us greater persistence.

Of course, the research has got a little further than just 'set goals' – performance can be improved even further if you set your goals in specific ways. Set goals for your academic efforts using the guidelines below. You can load up a text document and write them out on your computer, or copy out the worksheet in Appendix B if you prefer.

Distal and proximal goals

Distal and proximal goals simply means long- and short-term goals, respectively. Although it can be beneficial to set a distal goal, such as a specific GPA or other end-of-year grade, setting intermittent goals along the way has been shown to cause higher GPA than setting distal goals alone (e.g., Latham & Brown, 2006). Goals for each semester would be a good start but, ideally, you would include shorter time-periods, breakdowns for specific classes, assignments, and so on. If an essay deadline is a long way off, set proximal deadlines for different tasks, researching, planning, writing and editing (hint: set your final deadline a little earlier than the official one, then sit on your finished product for a day or two and check again). To help you identify suitable way-points to the distal goal, you can work from the goal backwards to your starting point, the other way around or both.

By the way, don't limit yourself to setting grade goals. Aside from your final grade, what else would leave you satisfied at the end of the course? Do you also want to build contacts, get a job at the university or master some subject areas in particular? Think about the subject areas that are the most relevant to you in terms of your future plans and aspirations or, if you don't yet have any, simply think about the areas of the course that appeal to you the most. Set goals to develop a deep understanding of these topics. If a class is relevant to your future career, a solid grasp of it will serve you well, regardless of your final grade (not least because it gives you plenty to talk about in job interviews).

Specific goals

One of the core findings of goal-setting research is that performance goals are more effective when they are specific and clear. A goal like 'Do well on my psychology course' or 'Do my best' will lead to a poorer performance than a goal like 'Achieve a 4.0 GPA' – all other things being equal of course. Make sure your goal makes clear the things that need to happen for you to have achieved it.

Bringing in specificity can be difficult with something more abstract like 'master this subject' but it is possible with a little thought. Think about what you'd be able to do if you achieved the abstract goal that you can't do now. For example for the 'master this subject' goal, you might set goals such as: read all the major papers and be able to summarize them without referring to them; form my own position on the field based on my own critique; pass my recall tests with 100 per cent accuracy; and so on.

Difficult goals

This is another core goal-setting principle. As long as the goal is within your ability to achieve (don't aim for a professorship by year 2!) and you're committed to it (e.g., you're on the right course, understand why you are doing psychology and what you want to get out of it), there is a linear relationship between the difficulty of a goal and both the effort put into it and the performance on the goal. Don't set easy goals that will just have you coasting along. Likewise, do not set goals that you do not truly believe you can achieve – your persistence will falter somewhere down the line. Research shows that goals lead to higher performance when they are difficult but achievable.

Learning goals

As this book should hopefully make clear, I have two main philosophies towards studying:

1. Create a deep understanding of the topics you will cover, particularly those that you are most interested in and intend to pursue further.
2. Learn studying as well as psychology.

Learning goals fall into category 2 and, according to one paper at least, lead directly to category 1 (Grant & Dweck, 2003). A learning goal involves making proactive efforts to improve your competence and generally involves learning new knowledge and skills to that end.

In complex tasks such as studying, it is generally not enough to set outcome goals. They are less effective and, in some cases, have been shown to be detrimental. On the other hand, learning goals are beneficial when the task is complex. In one study, MBA students who set learning goals ended with a higher GPA than students who set only distal goals and those who set the unspecific goal to 'do their best' (Locke & Latham, 2006).

What this means is that, as well as your goals of mastering the subject areas and achieving the grades you want, you should also set goals for the skills that will help you do these things. So goals to improve your reading, memory and any other the other methods covered in this book would apply perfectly. Normal goal rules apply to learning goals too – set proximal goals, make them specific and make them difficult.

Commitment

Although this might not be the most groundbreaking finding in the world, it has been demonstrated that goals lead to higher performance when commitment is high. To increase commitment, make your goal public. Tell your friends what you want to achieve each semester, post it on your social networks; generally, just tell people about it.

A second way to improve commitment is to improve your confidence in your ability to achieve the goal, which means training and skill-building in areas relevant to your goal. The other chapters in this book should give you ample material to do that.

Notice how these different techniques support and complement each other – learning to study gives you confidence, which gives you greater commitment. You can also tie your learning goals into your study skill development, which improves your overall performance, alongside your proximal and distal outcome goals.

Conflict

When two goals are in conflict, this can affect performance. You have possibly noticed this when your goal of completing that essay conflicts with your goal of having a good time on a Saturday night! But you might have other conflicts, everything from practical or logistical concerns about studying to philosophical problems with the nature of psychology and science. If it is simple, a matter of procrastination and motivation, this chapter will help. If you think empirical science is evil and want no part of it, that's a different matter. There isn't an easy answer to this and it will come down to an honest evaluation of what you want from life and the course. If you have persisted on the course and you are not excited or even interested in any of it, it might be worth taking some time to think about why that might be and what you are going to do about it.

Step 2 – Organization

Setting goals in the proper way will help you but their effects are subtle in that it is sometimes hard to attribute increased persistence and motivation on one day to a goal you set perhaps weeks ago. The same cannot be said of being organized and planning your time properly. This is something of which you will immediately notice the benefits.

What causes organization problems in students is the fact that 'studying' is not a task. It's a *concept*. If you 'go study', there are a million possible things that this could entail and if you don't know which one of those things you're going to tackle before you get to your desk, you'll waste time figuring it out: procrastinating by flicking through folders, opening and closing files, pushing papers around. Every productivity self-help book will tell you the same thing – set specific steps or 'next actions' that you have to take towards a larger goal (in our case, the closest proximal goal). Likewise, some prioritisation is needed to identify which area to focus on right now.

Organization

Effective organization boils down to having a system that tells you what you need to do, so you are never sat wasting time wondering what to get started on. The aim is to ease the self-regulation of your behaviour by passing control to your environment. If you want a specific and comprehensive system, a great book to get is Leo Babauta's (2007) short-but-sweet e-book, *Zen to done*, which you can download online for free and read in an hour or two. But whatever system you use, you will generally need the following things:

- inbox
- folders
- lists
- academic diary.

Inbox

Get yourself some form of inbox (any old tray will do) for your desk. Also, buy yourself a small memo pad so you can make quick notes of things to do. The inbox serves as a collection point for things you have to do – assignments, papers to look up, appointments – literally everything you have to do should move through this tray. Got a dentist appointment? Stick it in here. Your university gives you 3,000 forms to fill in? Into the tray with them. Have a spontaneous idea that you can't work on right now? Jot it down on the memo paper and drop it in the tray. You can use an equivalent electronic version of an inbox if you want but I prefer the analogue way because a lot of things have their own paper reminders anyway (an appointment slip, a letter, an assignment brief, and so on), and it's much easier just to chuck these in a tray to process later.

You may also wish to carry a notepad and pen wherever you go so that you can collect any thoughts and ideas you have while out and about. When you get home just tear the pages off and put them in the inbox for later processing.

Each day, you will go through the tray and make a decision on when and where you will act on each of these things. If it's only going to take a few minutes, do it then and there. If it's going to take longer, then either add a relevant next action to a list (see below for info on lists), or if it's a time-specific task like an appointment, put it in the diary.

Folders

Buy yourself a cheap pack of folders. If, for some reason, folders are ridiculously expensive where you live, you can buy some dividers and tape the edges together. Get one folder for each subject and put any handouts, printouts, papers, notes, mind maps or anything else that is relevant in there. If it starts to get too big, see if you can break it down further. For example, you might start with a cognitive psychology folder in which to keep all your notes and hand-outs but, when it gets too full, you start a new memory folder, then when that gets full you break it down by giving a different folder to different models of human memory, and so on. Use whatever system seems the most logical to you.

The goal is to have all your notes on a particular subject area in one place. When you sit down to study a topic, all the information you need will be there for you. There's really no need to waste time looking for that paper or handout – just reach for the folder. All it takes is a little investment in some cheap folders.

Hard drive folders

There are two ways you can organize your hard drive. One is to throw all your documents into one folder, unorganized, and then use your computer's search feature or a dedicated program such as Quicksilver to locate files quickly. This can work and it certainly saves time creating folders and dragging things around. But I don't advise it unless you're good at remembering the content of files or adding some kind of search phrase to them. Otherwise, you may have a tough time locating something specific. Additionally, some journal papers are not actually text documents but, rather, images of the text. These are not necessarily searchable, which can lead to headaches when locating them in this way.

Another advantage of having a logical folder system is that you can pull research together that you think might be related. Comparing and synthesizing separate fields of research is a great way to build, understand and strengthen your memory of a topic, so if you come across an article on evolutionary theory that you think relates to something you covered in developmental psychology, you can copy it into both folders. Then when you're doing research further down the line you'll be reminded of the paper.

Diary

Possibly the most essential item you can get is an academic diary. As mentioned above, every appointment, class and deadline goes in the diary. You can also put your distal and proximal goals in here too. If you are tenacious about filtering all the things you have to do through your inbox, you should never miss any time-specific task – assuming you check the diary every day. I repeat – you must make it a habit to check your diary every day, preferably at the same time of day, so that it's easier to make it habitual.

Lists

You have an inbox in which you can dump any ideas, tasks, assignment briefs or any other things that you'll need to do something about at some point. You also have a diary that notifies you of things you need to do at specific times. But what about the things that just need to be done 'at some point'?

They go on an old fashioned list. If you really want to, you can keep a list for each subject in the relevant folder but I think it's better to have a master list where actions for every subject and project go. The reason for this is that you can scan the master list and get an instant bird's eye view of your workload for the days and weeks ahead, which makes prioritising and planning easier. Items on the list should be *specific next actions* rather than vague ballpark statements about what to work on.

For example, imagine you need to prepare for your exams. 'Prepare for exam' is too general for a next action list, it makes it too easy to not do anything. What's the *very next single thing* you need to do to be prepared for the exam? That's what you put on the list. So, don't put 'Do research on cognitive psych' but, instead, 'Read through Baddeley (2000)'; don't put 'Revise for developmental exam', instead: 'Create recall tests based on attachment theory notes'. You get the idea – take the thought out of it, write an instruction you can immediately follow.

Step 3 – Planning

The above system is aimed at organising your materials and your tasks. The idea is that when you sit down to study, you're never stuck not knowing what to do. Planning is the process of taking the tasks that aren't time-bound (i.e., the things on your lists) and deciding when the best time to do them will be.

Review the list

To keep yourself up-to-date on what you have to do and what deadlines are approaching, go through your full list and look forward for a few weeks in your diary. Having a bird's eye view of all your upcoming actions and commitments will make it easier to prioritise. Do this at the end of the week; sometime during the weekend would be good.

Adding actions to the calendar

If you have followed the steps up to here, you should have a number of actions for each of your assignments, classes, learning goals, etc., plus a next action, and they should be written down somewhere. Although many of these tasks are not technically time-specific like a meeting is, they are in an indirect way because, if you leave them too long, you will get a backlog of studying to do when the exams draw nearer.

When you are looking over your lists and looking ahead, note any that must be completed in the week ahead. By this, I mean those that are essential, either because of a deadline or because they need to be done before you can get started on something else. Leo Babauta calls these the 'big rocks'. Put the big rocks in the diary for the week ahead. When you check your diary each day, you'll easily see whether you need to get to work on these or not.

Most important tasks for the day

As well as planning for the week ahead, you should also plan for the day ahead. You can do this in the morning or the evening before. First step, look at the calendar and see what's on there for the day. Because items only end up on your calendar when they are both essential and time-specific, these things get priority. If there are two or three things on there, you are probably set for the day and don't need to do any more planning. If not, go over your list and pick out two to three items for that day. You can either put them on a list and start working through them one-by-one or you can block out specific times to work on each task. Whatever works for you.

The principle of starting early

Here's something I bet you can relate to. The professor hands out the new list of essay titles. At the top of the page is the deadline – good, it's two months away. You think about which essay you might want to do and come up with a preference or maybe narrow it down to two options. You go home, put the brief somewhere and go switch on the TV. You've got two months, right? Plenty of time. No reason to start right away.

Six weeks later, you suddenly remember when the deadline is. You look for the brief and find it eventually under a pile of notes that you don't even remember writing. You put it on your desk, get a pen and then . . . go switch the TV on. Still two weeks left, right?

Sounds familiar? Don't worry; procrastination is a human universal. When you get an assignment with a fairly way-off deadline, it's human nature to procrastinate on it. But it is not the best way. Always start assignments early! If you can, choose an essay title *on the day that the options are given* and start looking for overview videos on TED [ted.com] and YouTube (see page 51) as soon as possible. Then make a list of the seminal papers to go through.

When you have a deadline ahead, set proximal goals and put them in your diary. Set deadlines to read those papers, write a plan and create a draft. It'll save you some stress later on.

Step 4 – Improving motivation and reducing procrastination

Many of the steps you've already taken will go a long way towards improving motivation and reducing procrastination. Setting goals with intermittent deadlines, being organized, planning your time; this will all help. But there are a few extra things we can do to give our motivation a boost. Some of these, as is common with the advice in this book, require a little up-front effort to pay dividends further down the line. Nowhere is this more important, however, than in this section. If you procrastinate on this, you may find yourself procrastinating even more later on!

The good things that will happen

One study found that people who take deliberate steps to make themselves aware of the benefits of achieving their goals will make better progress towards them. This does not mean fantasizing or daydreaming but making a clear list of benefits for each goal. For each of your distal goals outlined in Step 1, write a list of three to five benefits that will come once you have achieved this goal (see Wiseman, 2009).

Social support

The power of our social network on our own behaviour is a fascinating subject and worthy of a book in its own right. Researchers have found that if your best friend is obese, there is a 45 per cent chance that you are too; additionally, this cannot be fully explained by birds of a feather flocking together – friends actually influence each other (Christakis and Fowler, 2007). Closer to the point, other studies have hinted that college dorm-dwellers' GPA may be influenced by the GPA of their room-mates.

Clearly, social networks are important but I'm not suggesting that you pick your friends based on their academic ability! Your friends should be the people you like, of course; however, it certainly is useful to spend time with the high-fliers in your lectures. They usually sit at the front and ask lots of questions. Find these people and form study groups with them.

Dealing with procrastination

Procrastination is a tough thing to deal with, and it's very, very common. There might be a few genetic freaks out there that never procrastinate but they're the exception rather than the rule. Some days it's hard to bring yourself to do even the most simple of productive tasks! There are many reasons for this, including fear of failure, mental fatigue and plain old disliking of the task.

Luckily, there are many solutions too. Many of these solutions are built into the work on goal setting, planning and organization that you've already done – people who are organized and set goals tend to procrastinate less (e.g., Boice, 1989) – and some more solutions are also built into the techniques in the next section on decreasing distraction and increasing productivity. As well as this, though, another strong predictor of procrastination is the amount of *choice* that has to go into a task (Silver, 1974). The more choices you have to make, the more likely you are to put it off. I stressed this earlier; move the control of your behaviour to your planning system so you don't have to choose what to do every time you sit down to study. Micro-managing will only increase your choices and decrease your willpower.

Here are some more tips and tricks for dealing with procrastination:

- self-forgiveness
- work for two minutes
- don't just chase the grade
- piggybacking.

Self-forgiveness

Understand that procrastination is normal, happens to everyone at some point, and try not to give yourself a hard time about it. You're only human. In fact, one study found that students who forgave themselves for procrastination were less likely to procrastinate in the next semester. This wasn't an experimental design, so we don't know the cause and effect relationship but, at the very least, it seems like a safe bet that self-criticism over procrastination isn't going to help matters.

Work for two minutes

There is a simple trick that might help you to reduce procrastination. I know that when you're in that procrastinating mood you don't want to get started and any small task looks dauntingly large. So try telling yourself you'll get to work but only for two minutes. After that, you are free to stop working if you want. The idea is that this creates a kind of open loop in your mind, which increases the pressure to continue the task. The research on this is questionable and, from discussions with others, I note that it does not work for everyone. But, for some people, like me, it works almost every time. Since it doesn't cost anything to try, you might as well test it out.

Don't just chase the grade

I hope that this point is stressed to you throughout this book but getting a particular grade should not be your only goal in your course. It should be one of them, certainly, because a good grade opens doors and the challenge of pursuing it will develop many skills and qualities in you. But you should also be sensitive as to which areas of psychology are interesting to you, the ones you think about, that get you excited. What about your career or other life-aspirations, what can you draw from the field to help you towards these ends? Try to link these things into your work, wherever you can. The idea is that the more intrinsically motivating you can make studying, and the more meaning you can inject into it, the more you'll persist. Likewise, you won't see the course as being purely about the evaluation of your work because you have additional goals and intentions; Senecal *et al.* (1997) found that people are more likely to procrastinate on tasks when they expect to be evaluated.

Piggybacking

Ainslie (1992) proposes a rather clever way of avoiding procrastination that involves piggybacking the undesirable action on top of a desirable one. For example, if you're a social person, forming a study group where you get to discuss ideas and build relationships at the same time might really appeal to you and perhaps might not even feel like studying. Likewise, you might try studying in environments you like, such as in the park or other picturesque area. I found a good way to piggyback by starting a psychology blog through which I earn money from advertising. I research topics on my course and write them up into short blog posts, piggybacking study on to work. If you're technically minded you might piggyback by experimenting with various apps for your phone or computer, which you can adapt into study devices (such as a wiki). The exact piggybacking method you use will depend on what you consider to be 'not work', of course, so you'll have to experiment with this.

Step 5 – Improving performance on the task at hand

The final stage in this section on productivity concerns your actual performance when studying: what you can do to get more out of your time when you're actually sat down and ready to get started. Again, this section is not completely independent of the previous ones and your performance will be better if you have set goals, know what you need to do and are highly motivated. But by tweaking your 'at the desk' environment and behaviours, you can get even more out of your time.

Focus, rest and willpower

The principle to keep in mind is to work in 'blocks', which consist of 30–50 minutes of focused work, followed by 10–20 minutes of complete rest from work. In the work block, you solely, completely and intensely focus on the task you are working on. In the rest block, you do nothing intellectual at all. In doing so, you'll find that you get more done than if you had worked for long stretches at a time – unless the task you are doing required little mental effort.

The reason for this lies in the brain. Your ability to direct your attention takes energy; you will notice if you spend a long time on a hard mental task that you'll get hungry. And just like exercising a muscle, you can't sustain optimal effort continuously. If you don't take breaks:

- mental fatigue will set in
- you will find it harder to concentrate
- you will be more easily distracted
- your performance will tail off at some point.

If you do take breaks:

1. Your mental energy will be regularly restored (using the ideas below).
2. You will be less prone to distraction.
3. You will get more done.
4. You will be fresh again the next day.

In other words, it takes willpower to focus on a mentally challenging task. Willpower is finite – it runs out – and you need to take steps to replenish it between blocks of work.

Work blocks

On a work block, you work on your tasks and do *nothing else*. You do not check your phone. You do not check your email. You do not even blink unless I tell you to! (Sorry, I got carried away.) In a work block, you commit to working on the task you have set and you get on with it. In this modern age where so many things compete for your attention, you'll feel urges to open up Facebook or Twitter or to check your email but you won't pander to these urges. Once the work block is over, feel free to do what you like but, during the work block, it's focused effort only.

Use a timer for this. Any old timer with an alarm will do: on your computer, your watch, your phone; whatever. Set it for 30–50 minutes and then take 10–20 minutes as a break. I work for 40 minutes, then rest for 20 minutes but use whatever schedule you prefer. Not only will doing so improve your productivity but studies have shown that:

- regular breaks aid the learning of new information through something called the *primacy–recency effect* – so you are actually helping yourself to keep the information in.
- focused attention also improves recall – attention is essential to memory. If your attention is divided, the encoding of what you are learning into long-term memory is drastically impaired (Craik et al., 2000).

Rest blocks

Rachel and Stephen Kaplan have been researching mental fatigue for decades (e.g., Kaplan, 1995), and more recently Roy Baumeister and colleagues have made some excellent contributions (e.g., Muraven & Baumeister, 2000). The result is an impressive base of knowledge on what drains mental energy, and how it can be replenished. Here are some findings on the latter.

Aim for effortless attention on your breaks

Focused attention – the mentally draining kind – is consciously directed. *Effortless* attention is the opposite – anything that fascinates you, which draws you in without you having to focus on it deliberately. While your mind is engaged in effortless attention, the willpower reserves begin to replenish. So, on your break, doing something non-intellectual but fascinating will help restore your mental reserves. Spending time with children, pets, a computer game, even just lying back and daydreaming – as long as consciously directed attention is not being used, you'll reap some benefit (Kaplan, 1995).

Nature

A special note must go to nature because, as far as replenishing mental fatigue goes, there is vastly more evidence supporting natural environments than anything else (Kaplan, 1995). Benefits can come from a view of nature from a window, full immersion into a natural environment or even, incredibly, pictures of nature. If there's a garden or other green space near your work area, you'd do well to spend your break there. If you can't do that, maybe there's a wildlife documentary on TV.

Glucose

Willpower appears to use glucose for energy (Gailliot & Baumeister, 2007). When glucose is low, so is willpower. Keep this in mind when your stomach's rumbling and you're putting off getting something to eat. The quickest source of glucose of course would be energy drinks or non-diet soft drinks. Although I don't condone regular consumption of flavoured sugar-water, they might be useful for long exams, assuming you are not contraindicated.

A more sensible option, though, is small regular meals including complex carbohydrates and to keep taking breaks to allow your body time to convert them to glucose and transport them to the brain.

Affirming your core values

The use of glucose is a biological way to give self-control a little boost but a useful psychological method has been tested too. Self-affirmation refers to any event that bolsters a feeling of moral integrity and one of the ways that this can be done is by reflecting on our core values. In a serious of studies, participants who wrote about their top-ranked value and why it was important to them showed improved performance in a self-control task – but only when their willpower had been previously drained by a task that required focused attention (Schmeichel & Vohs, 2009). Participants only wrote for six minutes, so if you feel your willpower ebbing away, you might want to give this exercise a try.

Mindfulness meditation

Meditation may be another suitable way of replenishing attention. However, be aware of the specific type of meditation that you do. Some forms involve concentration, such as on the breath or on an object. These would involve directed attention and might drain your mental fatigue further. Other forms may be better suited; those that stress the open monitoring of experience – a present moment awareness without fixation on any stimuli in particular. For more information on the distinction between these forms of meditation, see Lutz, Slagter, Dunne and Davidson (2007).

Your productive environment

Whatever you are working on, get the relevant folder and put it on the desk. Clear the desk of everything that isn't relevant to that subject. Clutter and irrelevant books will only distract you.

If you are at the library and plan to cover three topics, get the books for them one topic at a time, even one book at a time unless there's only one copy on the shelf which you need to secure. Having a big pile of books just makes the task seem more daunting; it's much better to single-task. Plus you'll get to stretch your legs more.

How does your work area smell? There's a certain perfume that I smell occasionally which reminds me of an old friend from college every time. It seems pretty clear that smells can trigger memories that were encoded at the same time. There might be an advantage here in terms of wearing a certain perfume or aftershave while studying different subjects, then wearing the relevant one to that particular exam. I never tested this but it seems logical that it would work in practice.

Also relevant here is your internal environment. You probably know that physical exercise is good for your health. Did you also know it is good for the brain? Regular exercise can reduce the risk of dementia by 50 per cent (Laurin, Verreault, Lindsay, MacPherson, & Rockwood, 2001) and 20 minutes of aerobic exercise has been shown to improve our ability to learn new things and retain them (Winter et al., 2007). This isn't really a long time and you might find that your study sessions are enhanced as a result – not to mention the physical benefits.

Remove distractions

I spoke earlier about the importance of focusing on one task at a time. I repeat that here – single tasking is essential. There's even some evidence to suggest that rather than carry out two given tasks simultaneously, the brain switches very rapidly from one to the other (e.g., Rubinstein, Meyer and Evens, 2001). Even if this switching does happen incredible quickly, it doesn't seem like the most optimal way to go about things.

How this relates to performance isn't completely clear but what we do know is that people tend to make more mistakes when they are given two tasks to complete at once (Iqbal, Ju, & Horvitz, 2010). That just makes sense, doesn't it? When your attention is divided, you are more error-prone. On top of that, we know that when people are engaged in a task and then become distracted by something else, it can take on average ten minutes to resume the task and a further 10–15 minutes to return to the level of engagement experienced prior to the distraction! (Iqbal and Horvitz, 2007.)

All the more reason to work in blocks of intense, focused effort, followed by periods of rest and replenishment. Get your distractions out of the way while on your breaks and, while working, do nothing but focused work. Take the following steps during work blocks to remove distractions:

- Put a do not disturb sign on your door.
- Turn off your phone.
- Turn off your email program.
- Use a website blocker to restrict access to Facebook, Twitter, MySpace and any other websites that might distract you. There's a free program called *Self Control* that does this nicely. You put the websites on your blacklist, set the timer for however long you want, then run the program. You then cannot access these sites for that time period; even by closing the program or restarting your computer. Remember – take self-regulation of your behaviour out of the equation as much as you can and pass it to the environment.
- Practise! The temptation to lose focus will linger but you'll get better at ignoring it with time.

Don't do too much at once

As we've seen, self-control is drawn from a finite resource. That means, if you're on a diet, starting an exercise programme, learning Italian and working a day job at the same time as your psychology degree, you are going to be a little stretched, mentally. Keep in mind that, even with regular breaks, you will still need time in the evening to relax and recharge. Resist the temptation to do things that require directed attention all day long and set a point in the evening after which no more productive work is to be done. If you try to do too much in a day, you'll burn out quickly and your productivity will suffer, not to mention your wellbeing. If you are a workaholic, this might be hard to do but at least experiment with it and see if it works for you.

Find appropriate emotions for the job

Different emotions have different effects on our perceptions. So-called 'negative' emotions like fear, anger and anxiety tend to narrow our perceptions, as well as the thoughts and behaviours at our immediate disposal. 'Positive' emotions have the opposite effect and tend to broaden our perceptions and our thought–action repertoire. This is for survival purposes: negative emotions alert us to threats and narrow our responses so that we can deal with them; positive emotions alert us that things are going well and it is time to expand. However, we can also take advantage of this while studying.

Because 'negative' emotions tend to narrow our focus, they are appropriate for tasks that require attention to detail and focusing on the finer points. That would include a critical analysis of a paper, analyzing data, proofreading your essay; things like that. This is kind of a difficult point to make because I don't want you thinking that if you're in a good mood you have to ruin that just to do a critical evaluation – not at all. If you're in a good mood, feel free to stay that way! But this information might come into play when making certain decisions, such as what task to work on, or the music you put on; if you're proofreading, perhaps Chopin's *Nocturne* would sometimes be a better choice of study music than *Walking on Sunshine*.

On the other hand, if you are doing something that requires you to be creative, come up with new ideas, brainstorm or look at the big picture, positive emotions are more appropriate. Your performance is likely to be better if you do something to boost your mood beforehand – exercise, some good stand up comedy, a funny or uplifting YouTube clip – whatever works for you.

Track your progress

You shouldn't take anything you read in this book for granted (or any book, for that matter). The critical thinking mindset that you'll learn on your course (which we talked about from page 73 onwards), doesn't just apply to psychological research papers – it applies to everything. So while you should try this system out to see how effective it is for you, it would help if you found some way to track your productivity, so you can see exactly what effect it is having.

One way is to keep record certain metrics manually. If you're writing an essay, you could use the number of words written that day, if you're spending a day reading, you could use the number of pages read. You could use a diary and keep track of what you do and how long for, and compare the results before and after implementing these suggestions.

These ideas are well enough, but if you'd prefer an automated solution, I recommend RescueTime.com. Rescue Time is a program that runs in the background of your computer, which logs which windows are active and for how long and gives you a report at the end of the day. You can then find out exactly how long you've been spending working on your essay versus time spent on Twitter and email. It's a great way to get an objective measurement on your productivity but it's only useful when you're at the computer, of course. Rescue Time is not free for the full version but there is a free version that you can sign up to, which will do everything you need to run tests of these ideas – so you don't need to pay.

9 Conclusion

At this point, you've either made it through this whole book or you've read the bits you wanted and skipped to the end out of curiosity. Either way, I hope I've impressed upon you the idea that studying is a learnable skill. Succeeding on a degree course has very little to do with natural, innate talent and much more to do with the conscious actions you take. If you want to get a good grade and build a solid understanding of the subject, this is the attitude you should take towards your studies. No matter how difficult the course, a class, or an assignment might be, there's a skill you can learn that will help make it easier.

If you plan on following a career in psychology, the skills you'll learn within the major categories I've presented here will serve you throughout your whole career. But even if you don't, this is all very transferable, both in terms of the actual skills and the overall philosophy of the book itself. What you're doing is breaking a task down into its smaller, constituent parts and learning ways to improve your performance in these separate areas. This is something that will carry over to almost anything you want to do or learn; it's a great way of finding new, better ways to do things. If that's all you took from the book I'd be happy with that.

But I hope you will take more away than that. I accept that a certain percentage of people will read this book and not apply anything but I hope you won't be part of that category. I hope you apply these ideas and improve your grades and reduce your stress level.

It looks like goodbye, then. But, don't be a stranger; keep in touch with me at http://generallythinking.com.

Good luck with your studies!

Further reading

The following books will be useful to read after this one:

How to think straight about psychology by Keith Stanovich (superb, a must read for psych students).

Bad science by Ben Goldacre (great coverage of critical thinking and research methods issues; very engaging, with some brilliant real-life examples from Goldacre's efforts as a debunker).

Discovering statistics using SPSS: and (sex and drugs and rock 'n' roll) by Andy Field (excellent stats and research methods information; there's a version covering SAS, too, should you not use SPSS).

What is this thing called science? By A. F. Chalmers (getting deeper into philosophy of science, more technical and a denser read but probably the best book of its kind).

How to become a straight-A student: The unconventional strategies real college students use to score high while studying less By Cal Newport (the only study skills book I recommend, other than the one you are reading now).

Appendix A
Statistics cheat sheets

In these appendices you will find quick reference guides for reading and reporting the results of the statistical analyses we covered earlier. If you are reading a journal paper and need to know what something in the results section means, these will be useful to refer to until you get the hang of it. It won't be long until you can read the results of these tests without having to check what each symbol and number means but, in the meantime, it might be useful to photocopy them and pin them up on your wall.

Correlation

$$r = .45, p < .01$$

r is the test statistic for correlational data

p values indicate the result of a significance test

This is the probability of obtaining these results or greater by chance, assuming the null hypothesis to be correct. Look for values less than .05

The value of *r*, between −1 and 1. Figures below zero indicate a negative correlation, figures above zero indicate a positive correlation. Figures near zero indicate no correlation. Use these values as <u>guidelines:</u>

r = .3 (or −.3): weak correlation
r = .5 (or −.5): moderate correlation
r = .7 (or −.7): strong correlation

Regression

Regression and multiple regression are usually reported in tables.

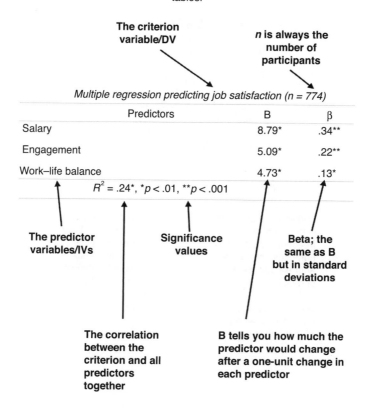

The criterion variable/DV

***n* is always the number of participants**

Multiple regression predicting job satisfaction (n = 774)

Predictors	B	β
Salary	8.79*	.34**
Engagement	5.09*	.22**
Work–life balance	4.73*	.13*

$R^2 = .24*$, $*p < .01$, $**p < .001$

The predictor variables/IVs

Significance values

Beta; the same as B but in standard deviations

The correlation between the criterion and all predictors together

B tells you how much the predictor would change after a one-unit change in each predictor

t test

$$t(66) = 5.674, p = .034$$

The value of *t* indicates the size of the difference between the means of two sets of data. Unlike *p*, there is no absolute value to look out for; it is more important to look at the effect size and *p*.

The figure in brackets is the degrees of freedom. For practical purposes, this is the approximate number of data points in the test. At degree level, you don't need to know about degrees of freedom in depth.

The *p* value tells you the probability of obtaining this mean difference or greater by chance, assuming the null hypothesis is correct.

ANOVA

$$F(2, 122) = 1.345, p = .034$$

The figures in brackets are degrees of freedom again. The first figure is the between-groups degrees of freedom (df); essentially, the number of groups minus one. The second figure is the within-groups df; for practical purposes, the approximate number of data points.

The p value again. It tells you the probability of obtaining this F value or greater by chance, assuming that the null hypothesis is correct.

The value of F. The greater the difference between the means of two or more groups in the analysis the greater the F value. Like the t statistic, there is no absolute value of F that you should look out for – consider effect sizes and significance levels instead.

Appendix B
Goal-setting worksheets

If you are finding that there is a little too much to take in with regard to the goal setting and productivity section of the book, you can use the cheat sheets ahead to make sure you've covered most of the bases. You don't have to use these, however, and if you know a better way or want to try your own ideas, that's fine too. It's intended that you use a separate sheet for each distal goal.

Goal-setting worksheet

Distal goal   **Target date**
_____ /_____

Delete as appropriate:

Learning goal/outcome goal

Proximal goals leading to this:

Goal	Target date	Tick

Checklist:

Goals are specific enough?	Yes / No
The goals are difficult but achievable?	Yes / No
Goal has been made public somehow?	Yes / No
I know the very next specific thing to do to make progress?	Yes / No
I've written that down on a list or on my calendar?	Yes / No

Benefits:

If I were to reach this goal, I would receive the following benefits:

1) _____

2) _____

3) _____

4) _____

5) _____

Contract:

If I find myself procrastinating on this I agree to at least work on the task for 2 minutes.	Yes / No
I will work in blocks of focused effort, interspaced by regular breaks where I do nothing intellectual.	Yes / No

Appendix C
American Psychological Association referencing cheat sheet

Use the guidelines ahead to help you reference your written assignments. Only the most common types of citation are in here; if you need to know how to format a reference that isn't covered here then go to the following web address:

flash1r.apa.org/apastyle/basics/index.htm
and see also the main APA style website:
apastyle.org/

APA Referencing – citing in-text

In the actual body of your document, all you need to do is give the surname and date of the author/s, so that the reader can look up the full details in the reference list. But there are some rules for how this is specifically done.

Single author

You can use any of these or similar varieties:

- 'Pinker (2002), notes that . . .'
- 'In 2002, Pinker suggested that . . .'
- 'The idea of the tabula rasa is no longer held in high regard by some researchers (Pinker, 2002).'

Two authors

If only the date is in brackets, use 'and' between the authors' names. If the whole citation is in brackets, use '&':

- 'Smith and Jones (2008) maintain that . . .'
- 'This finding has been replicated in subsequent tests (Smith & Jones, 2008).

Between three and five authors

The first time you cite the paper, give the names of each of the authors. In-text and parenthetical follow the same rules in terms of the use of 'and' or '&':

- 'Morgan, Mitsuka, and Doakes (2007) have argued that . . .'
- '. . . although this theory does not account for all previous findings (Malone, Crane, Peterson, Clavurn & Chambers, 1985)'

However, if you cite the paper again you should only give the name of the lead author followed by 'et al.'

- 'Morgan et al. (2007) propose that . . .'
- '. . . although the correlation was higher in other studies (Malone et al., 1985).

Six or more authors

When you have six or more authors, you can use the et al. version for every citation, including the first:

- 'Tribbiani et al., (2002) concluded that . . .'

Organisations and groups

If there is no associated author, just give the name of the associated organisation:

- 'For example, the University of East London (2001) notes that . . .'

If there's an abbreviation, give the full name first and the abbreviation afterwards:

- 'As noted in a report published by the National Health Service (NHS, 2006)'

In subsequent citations, just use the abbreviation:

- 'Although some action has been taken in this direction (NHS, 2006).'

APA Referencing – the reference list

The basic format for the reference list is like this for a journal:

- Surname, I. (year). Title of work. *Name of Journal. Volume no.* (issue no.), start page–end page (separated with an en dash).

And like this for a book:

- Surname, I. (year). *Title of work*. City of publishing, state/country: Publishing company.

Here are some examples:

Single author

- Baddeley, A. D. (2000). The episodic buffer: A new component of working memory? *Trends in Cognitive Sciences, 4*, 417–423.

Multiple authors

- Gruber, R., Laviolette, R., Deluca, P., Monson, E., Cornish, K., & Carrier, J. (2010). Short sleep duration is associated with poor performance on IQ measures in healthy school-age children. *Sleep Medicine, 11* (3), 289–294.

Book

- Pinker, S. (2002). *The blank slate: the modern denial of human nature*. New York, NY: Penguin.

Internet page

The website is the source, the web page itself is the article. A retrieved from date is technically only necessary where the webpage may change: which is most of them.

- Davies, W. (2009, June 16). Is time management important for students? *Generally Thinking*, Retrieved July 6, 2010, from generallythinking.com/why-is-time-management-important/

Chapter within an edited book

- Bergin, A. E., & Lambert, M. J. (1978). The evaluation of therapeutic outcome. In Bergin, A. E., & Garfield, S. L. (eds.), *Handbook of Psychotherapy and Behaviour Change*. New York, NY: Wiley.

When the author is an organization

- American Psychological Association. (2010). *Publication manual of the American Psychological Association* (6th ed.). Washington, DC: Author.

References

Ainslie, G. (1992). *Picoeconomics: The strategic interaction of successive motivational states within the person.* New York: Cambridge University Press.

Babauta, L. (2007). *Zen To Done: The simple productivity e-book,* Retrieved July 5, 2012 from zenhabits.net/zen-to-done-the-simple-productivity-e-book/.

Baddeley, A.D. (2000). The episodic buffer: A new component of working memory? *Trends in Cognitive Sciences, 4,* 417–423.

Benson, H. (1982). Body temperature changes during the practice of g Tum-mo yoga. *Nature, 295* (5846), 234–236.

Boice, R. (1989). Procrastination, busyness and bingeing. *Behaviour Research and Therapy, 27,* 605–611.

Buzan, T. and Buzan, B. (1996). *The mind map book: How to use radiant thinking to maximize your brain's untapped potential.* New York: Plume.

Byrne, B., & Davidson, E. (1985). On putting the horse before the cart: Exploring conceptual bases of word order via acquisition of a miniature artificial language. *Journal of Memory and Language, 24* (4), 377–389.

Chalmers, A. F. (1999). *What is this thing called science?* London: Hackett.

Christakis, N. A., & Fowler, J. H. (2007). The Spread of Obesity in a Large Social Network Over 32 Years. *New England Journal of Medicine, 357* (4), 370–379.

Craik, F.I., Naveh-Benjamin, M., Ishaik, G., & Anderson, N.D. (2000). Divided attention during encoding and retrieval: differential control effects? *Journal of Experimental Psychology: Learning, Memory, and Cognition, 26* (6), 1744–1749.

Diener, E., & Diener, M. (1995). Cross-cultural correlates of life satisfaction and self-esteem. *Journal of Personality and Social Psychology, 68,* 653–663.

Field, A. P. (2010). *Discovering statistics using SPSS (and sex and drugs and rock 'n' roll).* (3rd edn). London: Sage Publications.

Gailliot, M., & Baumeister, R. (2007). The physiology of willpower: Linking blood glucose to self-control. *Personality and Social Psychology Review, 11* (4), 303–327.

Goldacre, B. (2009). *Bad science.* London: Harper Perennial.

Grant, H., & Dweck, C. (2003). Clarifying achievement goals and their impact. *Journal of Personality and Social Psychology, 85* (3), 541–553.

Gruber, R., Laviolette, R., Deluca, P., Monson, E., Cornish, K., & Carrier, J. (2010). Short sleep duration is associated with poor performance on IQ measures in healthy school-age children. *Sleep Medicine,* 11 (3), 289–294.

Iqbal, S. T. & Horvitz, E. (2007). Disruption and recovery of computing tasks: field study, analysis, and directions, *Proceedings of CHI 2007, 677–686,* San Jose, California.

Iqbal, S.T., Ju, Y. C., & Horvitz, E. (2010). Cars, calls, and cognition: investigating driving and divided attention, *Proceedings of the ACM SIGCHI Conference on Human Factors in Computing Systems (CHI),* 1281–1290, Atlanta, GA.

Kaplan, S. (1995). The restorative benefits of nature: Toward an integrative framework. *Journal of Environmental Psychology 15* (3), 169–182.

Kashdan, T., & Breen, W. (2007). Materialism and diminished well-being: Experiential avoidance as a mediating mechanism. *Journal of Social and Clinical Psychology, 26* (5), 521–539.

Gueguen, N. (2007). Women's bust size and men's courtship solicitation. *Body Images, 4,* 386–390.

Harrington, N. (2005). It's too difficult! Frustration intolerance beliefs and procrastination. *Personality and Individual Differences,* 39 (5), 873–883.

Latham, G., & Brown, T. (2006). The effect of learning vs. outcome goals on self-efficacy, satisfaction and performance in an MBA program. *Applied Psychology: An International Review, 55* (4), 606–623.

Laurin, D., Verreault, R., Lindsay, J., MacPherson, K., & Rockwood, K. (2001). Physical activity and risk of cognitive impairment and dementia in elderly persons. *Archives of Neurology, 58,* 498–504.

Lett, J. (1990). A field guide to critical thinking. *Skeptical Inquirer,* 14 (4), 153–160.

Locke, E.A., & Latham, G.P. (2006). New directions in goal-setting theory. *Current Directions in Psychological Science,* 15, 265–268.

Lutz, A., Slagter, H., Dunne, J., & Davidson, R. (2008). Attention regulation and monitoring in meditation. *Trends in Cognitive Sciences, 12* (4), 163–169.

Muraven, M., & Baumeister, R. (2000). Self-regulation and depletion of limited resources: Does self-control resemble a muscle? *Psychological Bulletin, 126* (2), 247–259.

Newport, C. (2007). *How to become a straight-A student: The unconventional strategies real college students use to score high while studying less.* New York: Broadway Books.

Principe, G., & Smith, E. (2008). The tooth, the whole tooth and nothing but the tooth: How belief in the tooth fairy can engender false memories. *Applied Cognitive Psychology, 22* (5), 625–642.

Rockwood, K. (2001). Physical activity and risk of cognitive impairment and dementia in elderly persons. *Archives of Neurology, 58,* 498–504.

Rubinstein, J.S., Meyer, D.E., & Evans, J.E. (2001). Executive control of cognitive processes in task switching. *Journal of Experimental Psychology: Human Perception and Performance, 27* (4), 763–797.

Schmeichel, B.J., & Vohs, K.D. (2009). Self-affirmation and self-control: Affirming core values counteracts ego depletion. *Journal of Personality and Social Psychology, 96,* 770–782.

Senecal, C., Lavoie, K., & Koestner, R. (1997). Trait and situational factors in procrastination: An interactional model. *Journal of Social Behavior and Personality, 12,* 889–903.

Silver, M. (1974). Procrastination. *Centerpoint, 1,* 49–54.

Stanovich, K. E. (2009). *How to think straight about psychology.* New York: Allyn & Bacon.

Strohmetz D.B., Rind B., Fisher R. & Lynn M. (2002). Sweetening the till: The use of candy to increase restaurant tipping. *Journal of Applied Social Psychology, 32* (2), 300–309.

Truss, L. (2003). *Eats, shoots and leaves: The zero tolerance approach to punctuation.* London: Profile Books.

Vohs, K., Mead, N., & Goode, M. (2006). The Psychological Consequences of Money. *Science, 314* (5802), 1154–1156.

Winter, B., Breitenstein, C., Mooren, F., Voelker, K., Fobker, M., Lechtermann, A., et al. (2007). High impact running improves learning. *Neurobiology of Learning and Memory, 87* (4), 597–609.

Wiseman, R. (2009). *59 Seconds: Think a little, change a lot.* London: Pan Macmillan.

Index